Happily... Even After
Doing Marriage Right

Barry Stagner

Copyright © 2013 by Barry Stagner

Happily... Even After
Doing Marriage Right
by Barry Stagner

Printed in the United States of America

ISBN 9781626977440

All rights reserved solely by the author. The author guarantees all contents are original and do not infringe upon the legal rights of any other person or work. No part of this book may be reproduced in any form without the permission of the author. The views expressed in this book are not necessarily those of the publisher.

Unless otherwise indicated, all Scripture quotations are taken from the *Holy Bible*, New Living Translation, copyright © 1996, 2004, 2007. Used by permission of Tyndale House Publishers, Inc., Wheaton, Illinois 60189. All rights reserved.

Scripture quotations marked KJV are taken from the King James Version of the Bible.

Scripture quotations marked NASB are taken from the New American Standard Bible®, Copyright © 1960, 1962, 1963, 1968, 1971, 1972, 1973, 1975, 1977, 1995 by The Lockman Foundation. Used by permission.

Scripture quotations marked NIV are taken from the HOLY BIBLE, NEW INTERNATIONAL VERSION®. Copyright © 1973, 1978, 1984, 2011 by Biblica, Inc. Used by permission. All rights reserved worldwide.

Scripture quotations marked NKJV are taken from the New King James Version. Copyright © 1982 by Thomas Nelson, Inc. Used by permission. All rights reserved.

www.xulonpress.com

Dedicated to

Teri, Heather, Shane, Amber,

Tanner, Ava, and Ellie

Contents

Introduction v
Chapter 1: Marriage: Contract or Covenant?............... 9
Chapter 2: The Honeymooners 31
Chapter 3: Do You Hear What I Hear? 51
Chapter 4: What's Love Got to Do with It? 74
Chapter 5: The Rules of Combat 98
Chapter 6: In-Laws or Outlaws? 120
Chapter 7: When Everything Goes Wrong............. 144

Introduction

Among my favorite verses in Scripture are those of David in Psalm 19:7-11:

> The law of the Lord is perfect, converting the soul;
> The testimony of the Lord is sure, making wise the simple;
> The statutes of the Lord are right, rejoicing the heart;
> The commandment of the Lord is pure, enlightening the eyes;
> The fear of the Lord is clean, enduring forever;
> The judgments of the Lord are true and righteous altogether.
> More to be desired are they than gold,
> Yea, than much fine gold;
> Sweeter also than honey and the honeycomb.
> Moreover by them Your servant is warned,
> And in keeping them there is great reward. (NKJV)

The lessons here are many, yet the bar is set with the opening statement in verse 7. God's law is indeed perfect, and it is also sure, right, pure, enlightening, true and righteous, desirable, sweet, cautionary, and rewarding. Considering the issues of life that we all face, that sounds like something we might want to spend some time investigating, doesn't it?

In light of these verses, I have often said, "If your marriage is more like a battleground than a playground, you're doing it wrong." Accordingly, Malachi 2:11 describes marriage as "the Lord's holy institution which He loves" (NKJV). If, however, your marriage feels more like a penal institution or a mental institution, know today that God has provided in His Word instructions for how every marriage—even yours—can be a holy institution.

Anytime two imperfect people seek to join their lives in a holy union, there is bound to be a learning curve. That is normal and to be expected. Unfortunately, some couples never do learn, and the curve never straightens out. But even in those cases, the plan of God is still perfect.

The Bible's comparison of Jesus' love for the church to the husband-and-wife relationship is one of the greatest practical lessons we can apply to our marriages. Why? I'm glad you asked! One of the greatest lessons we learn from Jesus' love for the church is that no matter how we started out, no matter what we have done in the past, no matter how many mistakes we have made, God will still forgive and accept us as part of His bride. By extension to the husband-and-wife relationship, this means that no matter how your marriage started, no matter what has happened in it thus far, God has a plan that will allow you to live happily even after a bad start, a long string of mistakes, or repeated negative behavior.

But this book is not just for married couples. It is also a resource for dating couples or any "unclaimed blessings" out there waiting for Mr. or Ms. Right to come along. There are things to watch out for that indicate future problem areas, including some that are definite red flags that ought to give a person pause. I believe in the old adage "an ounce of prevention is worth a pound of cure." While the ordinance of marriage was made in heaven, people often make decisions regarding it without consulting the owner's manual, and they pay the consequences. Some good up-front wisdom will help anyone who is single and in the process of selecting a mate, which is the second most important decision in a person's life.

Whether you are interested in having a great marriage, repairing a broken one, or starting out right in one, who better to consult than the founder of the institution whose comments on the matter are perfect, sure, right, pure, enlightening, true and righteous, desirable, sweet, cautionary, and rewarding. Before you begin, however, let me give you one more word of encouragement from the founder of the institution of marriage.

In John 13:17, Jesus said, "If you know these things, blessed are you if you do them" (NKJV). God loves marriage, and He has provided instructions that will allow any marriage to be blessed, even after a shaky start. But we have to do them, not just read about them. To any of you who may be thinking, "You're a pastor. What do you know about real marriage struggles?" let me say this: my marriage is as real as anybody's, and my wife and I are two fallible people trying to follow the plan of a perfect Savior. But the fact is, the perfect plan must be applied by anyone who enters this holy institution that God loves in order for their marriage to be the blessing God intended it to be.

I hope you'll decide today to take God's perfect plan for marriage to heart. May the Lord bless you as you read and apply the biblical truths in this journey of living *happily . . . even after!*

Chapter 1

MARRIAGE: CONTRACT OR COVENANT?

*Then the L*ORD *God said, "It is not good for the man to be alone. I will make a helper who is just right for him."*

—GENESIS 2:18

A young couple decided to write their wedding vows. On the day of the big event, they stood face-to-face in front of me and declared before all their deep affection for each other. Then, at the conclusion of all the flowery affirmations, the soon-to-be husband and wife pledged their mutual commitment with the words "as long as our love lasts." Talk about setting yourself up for failure!

Yes, love is indeed a many-splendored thing, as the young couple professed, but it is also a lifelong commitment that requires much hard work in the inevitable struggles and challenges of life that will arise. If your commitment to your marriage extends only "as long as our love lasts," and love to you is simply how you feel, rest assured, the time will come when love seems absent and the temptation to flee is overwhelming. That's the time when only a commitment made on something greater than the feeling of love will be sufficient to sustain the relationship.

But that is exactly one of the reasons so many marriages are failing today. We lack understanding of what marriage truly is and mistakenly assume the *feeling* of love is the barometer we use to measure the health of our marriage. If the feelings of passion and excitement cool (though they don't have to), we conclude that the marriage is dead and we are free to leave. That might be true if marriage were nothing more than a contractual obligation based on mutual benefit that could be dissolved when both parties agreed the arrangement was no longer beneficial. And sadly, that is just the view many people today — even some within the church — hold of what was once known as the "sacred institution of marriage."

But marriage is not a contractual agreement, my friend. It is a covenant made between one man and one woman before God, and that puts it on an entirely different level. To boil it down to a legal contract cheapens it and almost certainly sets the scene for failure. To raise it to the level of covenant, however, affirms it sacredness and greatly increases the chance of its success. That's what this first chapter of *Happily . . . Even After* is about — the covenant of marriage and what that means to you and me right where we live today.

Now, I realize not all of you reading this book are married, and that's okay. The apostle Paul addressed both single people and married couples in 1 Corinthians 7:8-9, explaining that both states are callings from God and that we are to accept the one we have received. God has not called the single to their single lives against their wills, and neither has He called the married against their wills. He gives grace to both in their respective callings. The key lies in knowing your calling and accepting it.

Others of you reading this book are single, but not by choice. You long for that special someone to go through life with. Or maybe you have already experienced that, until the cruelty of divorce ripped it from your hands and your dreams lay shattered at your feet. And some of you were privileged enough to share a rich and meaningful marriage with a spouse who has since gone home to be with the Lord, and you would like to experience that again.

Whether you have never been married, are currently married, or were once married but now find yourself single, there is something for you in *Happily . . . Even After.* You can learn how to do marriage right, how to do it God's way. It all begins with understanding God's intention for marriage and grasping the fundamental principle that marriage is a *covenant*, not a *contract*.

God's Original Intent

Two women went to lunch one day. One of the women noticed something odd about her friend and commented, "You're wearing your wedding ring on the wrong finger." To that her friend quickly replied, "That's because I'm married to the wrong man!"

We may laugh at that little joke, but friends, the vast majority of marital problems—despite what we may think—are not because we're married to the wrong person, but because we're following the wrong plan. We're ignorant of God's original intent for marriage or choose to follow our own plan instead. We push "for better or for worse, for richer or for poorer, in sickness and in health, until death do us part" to a far corner of our mind where it will make no demands on our selfish desires. We'd much rather pledge fidelity, trust, and commitment "as long as our love shall last," rather than "until death do us part." But that is not God's plan, and that perspective will never bring us what we're looking for in this earthly life. Only when we examine again and take as our own God's original intent for marriage and commit to doing it right will we achieve a marriage that is "happily even after" — even after unmet needs, crushing disappointment, or unspeakable tragedy rears its head and threatens the foundation of our married life.

Psalm 18:30 announces, "God's way is perfect. All the LORD's promises prove true. He is a shield for all who look to him for protection." God's way for marriage is perfect. For those who will dare to believe Him, all His promises are true: You *can* have a life-affirming relationship with your spouse. You *can* build a love that will weather the storms of life and the disappointment of unfulfilled dreams and unmet potential. You *can* journey through life with a companion who completes you, complements your weaknesses, and enhances your strengths. You *can*, most assuredly, live happily even after in the great adventure called marriage. But it all begins with understanding and embracing God's plan.

So, if marriage was made in heaven — and it was — and if the Word of God is true — and it is — then we certainly want to take a look at what God says about it in the Bible. That means going back to the beginning, to the book of Genesis. After God created the heavens and the earth, the animals, and man himself, He looked upon His work and proclaimed it good. He established a lush garden and placed the man within it to tend it and watch over it. But then, in Genesis 2:18, God made a very interesting observation: "It is *not good* for the man to be alone" (emphasis added). God found something that was "not good" in His wondrous creation, and it was the fact that man was alone. Immediately God initiated His plan: "I will make a helper who is just right for him" (v. 18).

In the next two verses of Genesis 2, verses 19 and 20, we see God bringing the animals before Adam for him to name. I don't believe it's too far a stretch to assume that they came before him in pairs, but "there was no helper just right for him" (v. 20). I believe in this Adam learned something very important: neither his work nor his dominion over creation could fully satisfy him. Something was missing, and he would remain incomplete unless God intervened.

And intervene He did—putting Adam to sleep and removing a rib from his side to fashion a perfect helpmate. Then he brought her to Adam. Listen to Adam's pure, unadulterated joy when he opened his eyes to the scene before him: " 'At last!' the man exclaimed. 'This one is bone from my bone, and flesh from my flesh! She will be called "woman," because she was taken from "man" ' " (v. 23). In his words "At last!" is the fulfillment of his longing. I can almost hear Adam saying, "Now that's what I'm talkin' about!"

Then, the culmination of God's plan is seen in verse 24: "This explains why a man leaves his father and mother and is joined to his wife, and the two are united into one." Jesus quoted this verse in the Gospels and the apostle Paul in Ephesians. It is the foundation for all marriage and the starting point for our study.

Included in this passage from Genesis 2 is the need to recognize basic man-woman differences and the acknowledgment that these differences are of divine origin. There was a lot of stuff in the rib that was removed from man and placed in woman. Take the shopping gene, for instance. Obviously, Eve got the bulk of that "talent," as seen in the distinctive ways most men and women approach shopping. For men, the process looks like this: acquire target, secure target, return to base. I can testify from experience that when I go shopping with my wife, we look at things we didn't go to the mall for, we come home with things I didn't know we needed, and we buy things just because they are on sale in order to save money on them. (My male brain says we could save a lot more by leaving this stuff at the store, but I don't mention that to my wife!) These differences between male and female are not wrong—they're just different. Nonetheless, basic male-female differences are often the source of big problems in marriage and therefore need to be addressed.

Here's a point to recognize first and foremost as we begin our study of doing marriage right:

Marriage is the solution — not the problem.

When God declared Adam's aloneness as "not good," He immediately solved the problem by creating Eve. Marriage is God's *solution* to a problem, not the *cause* of it. That's an important point to grasp. Your marriage is intended to be the solution to a problem—not the cause of creating even bigger ones!

When God sees that something is not good and then creates a solution, as He did when He gave Eve to Adam, then how can the thing created as the solution so often seem like the problem? The answer is, the problem lies not in the solution, but in the people involved. *We* are the problem in our marriage—not the marriage itself. *We* are the ones who have deviated from God's plan—not, as some claim, that the plan is inadequate and irrelevant in today's world.

I once heard the story of a mild-mannered man who became tired of his wife always bossing him around, so he went to a psychiatrist who gave him a book on being assertive. On the train ride home that day, he read the first chapter and decided to try out the actions suggested.

Walking in the door of his home, the man announced to his wife, "From now on, I am the man of this house, and my word is law. When I get home from work, I want my dinner on the table. Now I want you to go upstairs and lay out some clothes for me because I am going out with the boys tonight. After that, draw me a bath. And when I get out of the bath, guess who's going to help me get dressed!"

Looking her husband full in the face, the woman calmly responded, "The undertaker."

We're all guilty of trying to force our mate into a desired image rather than accepting him or her as the other half of ourselves. It's far too easy to see our spouse as the problem rather than to acknowledge that maybe we, too, need to change. It's often tempting to think that marriage is the cause of all our problems, when in reality God gave it to us as a solution to our problems.

The plan of God is good and does not create problems. If we are experiencing problems in our marriage, the truth is, we are not doing marriage right and are not following God's plan. If we're going to get anywhere in our understanding of marriage, then we must first recognize that no Christian marriage need ever fail. As a matter of fact, marriage can be a fantastic, joyous experience, even though entered into by two fallible people. As Proverbs 5:18 exhorts, "Let your wife be a fountain of blessing for you. Rejoice in the wife of your youth." And Proverbs 18:22 adds, "The man who finds a wife finds a treasure, and he receives favor from the LORD." That's the truth of Scripture, and that can be the reality of your married life once you understand that marriage is the solution — not the problem.

Life is a battleground, but marriage is meant to be a playground with only an occasional battle to resolve. Marriage is meant to be a joy, and it is God's good solution to the one thing He saw in creation that was "not good" — man's aloneness. This is God's plan, and you should absolutely expect marriage to be every bit as wonderful as everything else that God has made.

I can almost hear some of you saying, "Pastor, you're living in a dream land. You don't know how tough marriage can be." I understand where you're coming from, because I've been there. I've lived in a marriage that I made into a hell. I ignored the God-ordained differences between men and women and paid the price for it. I failed to love my wife as Christ loves the church. As a matter of fact, when my wife and I entered marriage, neither of us was walking with the Lord, and we were both ignorant of God's plan.

But thankfully, there's another side to my story. I am also one who knows that God's plan works no matter when you begin to obey it. Anytime a couple starts doing marriage right, God can turn a marriage that is a living hell into a little taste of heaven. That can be your story too, and that's why I'm writing this book. I want you to learn how to live happily even after — after the memory of the vows fades, the excitement of new love wears off, and normal everyday life takes over.

Let's go back to the original emphasis of this chapter, marriage as a covenant. Remember, marriage is not a contract, a series of legal obligations that when unmet release the parties from further continuance. No, marriage is a covenant, holy and sacred, instituted by God Himself. Let's look into Scripture and see what it says about this.

God's Call to Faithfulness

In Malachi 2:11, we read, "Judah has been unfaithful, and a detestable thing has been done in Israel and in Jerusalem. The men of Judah have defiled the LORD's beloved sanctuary by marrying women who worship idols." The men of Israel committed spiritual adultery by marrying pagan women and accepting their gods. We must understand that God was not concerned with keeping the Jewish people racially pure, but He was overwhelmingly concerned with keeping them spiritually pure. There is but one race, the human race, but when the men of Israel intermarried with pagan women, they allowed their human relationship to pollute their spiritual relationship with God.

This same idea of spiritual purity is repeated in the New Testament: "Don't team up with those who are unbelievers. How can righteousness be a partner with wickedness? How can light live with darkness? What harmony can there be between Christ and the devil? How can a believer be a partner with an unbeliever?" (2 Cor. 6:14–15). Both Malachi and the apostle Paul are dealing with the same issue: the need for God's people to be yoked in marriage only with those who also profess belief in the one true God. To do otherwise is not only unwise but also unscriptural.

Young people and all singles, listen to me. Dating is not a sport. It's the process of selecting a mate and should be treated as such. Passions run high in male-female relationships, and when you put yourself in situations that you are too young or unprepared to handle, you are taking a great and unnecessary risk of falling prey to lust and other natural temptations. If you are not yet ready for marriage, then dating as we know it in American culture is not in your best interests. "But," you might protest, "isn't dating the way to find out what qualities I want in a mate and whether a particular person might be a suitable spouse?" It's true you have to get to know a person, but that's best accomplished, in the initial stages at least, in group settings that provide safe social contact. But even that is prefaced by the assumption that the person you are interested in is a believer.

Now for those who may be thinking that I am out of touch with culture and modern pressures, remember, it doesn't matter what we think; it's what God says about a matter that is important. This includes His instruction concerning the interaction of unmarried people of opposite sexes. Culture doesn't define morals and standards—God does.

For you who are looking for Mr. or Ms. Right, keep in mind that dating a nonbeliever is nothing less than disobedience to God. He has made His will clear in both the Old and New Testaments. If you insist on dating a nonbeliever, you expose yourself to that person's gods, the things they hold dear, and that can range anywhere from lust to false religion.

In God's plan of covenant marriage, the first issue to be settled in our minds is that Christian marriage is between two believers. "Missionary dating" has no place in God's family. Dating is not the place for personal evangelism. Human nature being what it is, it is always easier to be pulled down to another's level than to pull someone else up to your level. The wise person knows this and refuses to compromise his or her faith by entering into dating relationships with nonbelievers.

Now, back to Malachi 2. Let's read verses 13–16 in the New American Standard Bible:

This is another thing you do: you cover the altar of the LORD with tears, with weeping and with groaning, because He no longer regards the offering or accepts it with favor from your hand. Yet you say, "For what reason?" Because the LORD has been a witness between you and the wife of your youth, against whom you have dealt treacherously, though she is your companion and your wife by covenant. But not one has done so who has a remnant of the Spirit. And what did that one do while he was seeking a godly offspring? Take heed then to your spirit, and let no one deal treacherously against the wife of your youth. "For I hate divorce," says the LORD, the God of Israel, "and him who covers his garment with wrong," says the LORD of hosts. So take heed to your spirit, that you do not deal treacherously.

Once we are married — and hopefully to a fellow believer — the Lord's plan is that we remain together. Look carefully at verse 14 above: "She is your companion *and your wife by covenant*" (emphasis added). God makes it clear that marriage is a covenant relationship. In a contract, the parties involved establish the conditions by which the contract remains in effect. Together they mutually agree to these terms. In God's covenant of marriage, however, the conditions are not established by the man and the woman, but by a third party — God Almighty. The man and the woman willingly enter into agreement with God's covenant conditions. When this concept is embraced, the power of Ecclesiastes 4:12 is unleashed: "A person standing alone can be attacked and defeated, but two can stand back-to-back and conquer. Three are even better, for a triple-braided cord is not easily broken." In God's plan of marriage, man, woman, and God form a threefold cord that can withstand even the most difficult trial that might come their way.

I don't know why we have such a hard time believing God's way is best. Somehow we think we know better and can dictate our own plan, assuming God will bless it anyway. But that's not the way it works.

A groom approached the pastor at his wedding rehearsal in order to slip him a hundred-dollar bill and make a request. "Pastor," he asked, "I'd sure appreciate it if you would skip the part about promising to love and obey and be faithful unto death." The pastor said nothing, but took the bill.

On the day of the wedding, when the time arrived for the exchange of vows, the pastor looked at the groom and said, "Will you promise to prostrate yourself before this woman, obey her every command, serve her breakfast in bed, and swear before God and these witnesses that you will never look at another woman as long as you both shall live?"

Taken aback, the young groom gulped and said, "I will." But then he leaned toward the pastor and whispered, "What happened? I thought we had a deal."

The pastor fished in his pocket, leaned toward the young man, and replied, "Here's your money back. She made me a better offer!"

Friends, you can rewrite the wedding vows all you want, but the covenant conditions are divine and will never change.

Covenantal Covering

Much as we give an engagement ring to pledge our commitment to a future wife, a Jewish man in biblical days had his own way of showing his commitment to his future bride. A man would cover his bride with his garment, signifying his desire to enter into covenant relationship with her and offer her his protection. It was a symbolic act recognizing the covenant conditions of the ordinance of marriage.

We see this practice at work in the story of Ruth in the Old Testament. After Ruth returned to Israel with her mother-in-law, Naomi, the older woman set into motion a plan to obtain a husband for Ruth and security for both her and her daughter-in-law. She instructed Ruth to visit a near kinsman, Boaz, on the threshing floor, and Ruth did as she was told. In Ruth 3:7-9, we read:

> After Boaz had finished eating and drinking and was in good spirits, he lay down at the far end of the pile of grain and went to sleep. Then Ruth came quietly, uncovered his feet, and lay down. Around midnight Boaz suddenly woke up and turned over. He was surprised to find a woman lying at his feet! "Who are you?" he asked.
> "I am your servant Ruth," she replied. "Spread the corner of your covering over me, for you are my family redeemer."

Boaz covered the young woman with his garment, and shortly thereafter he completed the necessary requirements to take Ruth as his wife.

Through the prophet Malachi, God said to the men of Israel and to us today that He hates divorce because it violently rips the covering from his covenant daughters: " 'For I hate divorce,' says the Lord, the God of Israel, 'and him who covers his garment with wrong,' says the Lord of hosts. So take heed to your spirit, that you do not deal treacherously" (Mal. 2:16, NASB). Divorce breaks the covenant, and that is not something God takes lightly.

The word "treacherously" in the verse above is interesting in this context. It means "to pillage under the covering." When men deal "treacherously" with their wives, they are wreaking havoc and destruction under the ruse of being the heads of their homes, and they are pillaging the hearts and lives of those they have sworn to protect. Yes, God hates divorce, for it takes a divine ordinance meant to provide covering and turns it into an act of violence. Don't ever take that lightly, and never forget this next major point:

Breaking the covenant conditions is to reject God's plan.

To break God's covenant conditions of marriage is to reject God's plan, and how can we expect to experience the covenant blessings when we do that? God indeed hates it when a marriage comes to an end, but that is not the only thing being spoken of in Malachi 2:16. God also hates it when, although a marriage remains legally intact, the holy institution becomes a place of pillage under covering. Men, you are the head of your household; nothing can change that. And women, you are called to submit to your husband in this capacity. Scripture makes the marital relationship clear in Ephesians 5:21–25:

> Submit to one another out of reverence for Christ.
> For wives, this means submit to your husbands as to the Lord. For a husband is the head of his wife as Christ is the head of the church. He is the Savior of his body, the church. As the church submits to Christ, so you wives should submit to your husbands in everything.
> For husbands, this means love your wives, just as Christ loved the church.

Dear friends, God hates it when the covenant conditions are not lived out in any home. He hates it when men do not love their wives as Christ loved the church and when women in turn refuse to acknowledge their husbands' role and willingly submit to them.

Let me address the men for a minute. Men, how can you expect your wife to live up to her end of God's covenant if you have not lived up to your end of the covenant conditions? Your role is to love your wife as Christ loved the church, who humbled Himself and became a servant, who denied His own rights and relinquished His power for the benefit of His bride. Jesus loves the church amidst all her failures and shortfalls. He loves His bride on her good days and bad days, in sickness and in health, for better or for worse. There is not a Christian woman in the world, I believe, who would not willingly submit to love like that.

Marital problems do not arise from two people trying to become one. In the eyes of God, that work is accomplished when they say "I do." Marital problems arise when one tries to live like two, when husband and wife each insist on their own way rather than submitting to each other as unto the Lord. Men, are you loving your wife as you are called to do, or have you tried to write your own covenant conditions? Ladies, are you living under the arrangement God has set for the home, or have you set your own conditions? For both men and women, breaking the covenant conditions as established by God grieves His heart because it is a rejection of His divine plan.

If we stopped here in our study, we would be stopping short of understanding the full truth of God's wonderful plan for marriage. If we stopped here, we might gain the skewed perspective that no matter what, we have to put up with a bad marriage. If we stopped right here, we might come away with a negative perspective of a sacred covenant.

It is true that God hates divorce because He knows what it does to the two who have become one. He loves them and has a better plan than what they have settled for. In Him, even bad marriages have the potential to become great ones. In Mark 10:1–12, Jesus made clear the sanctity of marriage and the Father's desire for it to be permanent. But in a corresponding verse, Matthew 5:32, He did allow one concession for the dissolution of a marriage: "But I say to you that whoever divorces his wife for any reason *except sexual immorality* causes her to commit adultery; and whoever marries a woman who is divorced commits adultery" (NKJV, emphasis added).

The phrase "sexual immorality" is the Greek word *porneo*, from which we get the English word *pornography*. Reality TV has presented a rather sad view of relationships today, especially in the area of sexual faithfulness. But contrary to what we see on TV or look at on the Internet, God requires sexual faithfulness in marriage and sexual purity in those who are single. He even requires it in thought and sight, for the eyes and mind are the things that fuel the fire of unfaithfulness. And when that faithfulness is betrayed, God does allow divorce.

Keep in mind, however, that the couple does not *have* to get divorced. The devastation resulting from sexual immorality can be overcome, and a couple can live happily even after encountering such a huge trauma. I have seen this happen time and time again. But sometimes in this fallen world, the betrayal is so great and so damaging that some hearts are irreparably broken, and trust is lost for good. The truth is, a relationship with no trust is no relationship at all, so when trust is irreparably broken through infidelity, God provides a way out.

Benefits of Living under Covenant Conditions

The messed-up, jumbled-up interpretation of marriage that we see today is not how it was meant to be. It is not God's original design for the holy institution of marriage. We need to remind ourselves often of His purposes as written in His Word: "It is the same with my word. I send it out, and it always produces fruit. It will accomplish all I want it to, and it will prosper everywhere I send it" (Isa. 55:11). This word applies to your marriage. No matter how broken it may seem, God has spoken His word over it and promises you that it will accomplish what He has planned. Now that's something to shout about!

Marriage: Contract or Covenant?

In Mark 10:9, the Bible says, "What therefore God hath joined together, let not man put asunder" (KJV). The phrase "put asunder" is the Greek word *chorizo*, which means "to place room between." The instruction is clear: do not minimize God's plan for marriage by regarding it as a contract rather than a covenant. The implication, however, extends even further. In marriage, we are not to allow any room for the thought that "my marriage is beyond repair," or "my marriage is beyond hope." It is a firm declaration that nothing, when submitted to almighty God, can tear asunder what God has joined together.

My question to you is, have you tried doing marriage right, meaning God's way? Singles, do you have high expectations for the person you will spend the rest of your life with? That begins with expecting to spend the *rest of your life* with that person. God's plan works every time, and His words regarding marriage will not return empty but will produce the promised fruit and achieve His divine purpose when we obey them.

Can anyone have an awesome marriage? Yes, anyone who lives by the covenant conditions, that is. Does that mean a Christian marriage will be without problems? Does it mean that every day will be a honeymoon, that you will feel nothing but the exhilaration of love for your spouse all day every day? Does it mean you will never fight, and if you do, then you must have failed? All those questions and more will be answered in the following chapters.

Let me wrap up this chapter with Isaiah 61:3-4: "To all who mourn in Israel, he will give a crown of beauty for ashes, a joyous blessing instead of mourning, festive praise instead of despair.

In their righteousness, they will be like great oaks that the Lord has planted for his own glory. They will rebuild the ancient ruins, repairing cities destroyed long ago. They will revive them, though they have been deserted for many generations."

Brothers and sisters in Christ, if your marriage seems like ashes, know that God has a crown of beauty waiting for you. He has a joyous blessing to replace the mourning of lost love, and He will even rebuild the ruins of your life to the repair of future generations, your children.

If you are just beginning your years as a couple, make sure you are using the Word of God as a compass for your journey together. If you start on a long trek with your compass one or two degrees off, the longer you travel, the farther off track you will become. Start right and you'll finish right, and everything in between will be on track as well.

Friends, listen, meeting covenant conditions cannot yield unsatisfactory results. The Word of God applied to any marriage will not—cannot—return empty, but it *will* produce the fruit that God has promised. And that is the fruit of two people, one man and one woman, made one flesh under the covenant conditions of a holy God.

Marriage—is it a contract between two human beings or a covenant with a holy God? Your answer to that question may well determine the future of your marriage. But as for me, I have fully embraced the fact, as stated in God's Word, that marriage is a holy institution with conditions attached, a divine plan that assures every couple that their marriage can be filled with all the good things God intended in His original design.

Questions for Discussion

Principle

Marriage is not a contractual agreement. It is a covenant made between one man and one woman before God. That puts it on an entirely different level. Boiling it down to a legal contract cheapens it and almost certainly sets the scene for failure. Elevating it to a God-given principle of covenant restores its sacredness and greatly increases its chance of success.

Personal

Take a few moments to examine your heart. Be honest with yourself about what you really believe regarding marriage.

How have you defined marriage? Does your view of marriage line up with God's?

- Do Christian marriages have an advantage over other marriages? If so, what are they?

Have you been seeing your marriage as a problem rather than as the solution God meant it to be?

- Have you entertained the thought of divorce as a viable option even though you have no scriptural grounds for it?

- Why is divorce such a serious action in the eyes of God? What is the only scriptural grounds for divorce? How does this differ from what we see in the world around us?

- Can the right person seem like the wrong person at times? What basic differences between husbands and wives are part of any marriage?

Singles, have you been enticed by the world's standards and wavered from God's plan to date only fellow believers?

- Why is being "equally yoked" important when considering a prospective mate?

Purposeful

Commit in your heart to being purposeful, elevating your thoughts and beliefs regarding marriage—your marriage—to God's standard.

Remove from your speech the use of the word *divorce*, and don't allow yourself to say things like, "This just won't work," "I can't do this anymore," or "I know what God's Word says, but my marriage is the exception."

Think about and meditate on what marriage really is.

Prayer

Dear heavenly Father, I thank You for Your heart towards marriage, my marriage. I ask that you heal my mind and heart as I journey with You through *Happily . . . Even After*. Please help me see marriage as You see it. I ask You to give me courage to believe Your Word as I choose to obey it even when I do not feel like it. I ask that You give me a heart that grows deeper in love with You and with my spouse. In Jesus' name I pray. Amen.

Chapter 2

The Honeymooners

Above all, clothe yourselves with love, which binds us all together in perfect harmony.

— Colossians 3:14

Once the foundation of marriage as a covenant has been established, there is still the reality of living out this divine covenant in a temporal world. Just because we agree with God that marriage is a holy institution does not mean we automatically know how to act in it in the most life-affirming ways. We are, after all, mere "earthen vessels," carrying the glory of God within our flawed human forms (see 2 Corinthians 4:7, NKJV).

The early days of a married couple's relationship is often known as the honeymoon period. Life is indeed as sweet as honey during this idyllic period. Conflict is minimal and easily resolved. Selfishness is submerged to selflessness for the spouse's every need. The future is bright with endless tomorrows of unabated joy and pleasure beckoning on the horizon. Most married people experience something similar in the early days of their marriage, but few expect it to last past the initial months of the new relationship. That's sad, but true; however, I believe marriage is meant to be a honeymoon—period. I don't believe we have to accept an inevitable decline in this special relationship. Marriage done right, as a covenant relationship, can be a continual honeymoon as long as the husband and wife are both committed to living according to the covenant conditions. Remember, God doesn't just hate the act of divorce; He also hates it when we fail to live out our marriages according to the covenant conditions, because it robs His children of His intended marital blessings and exposes them to the pain of separation or divorce.

The covenant conditions that allow us to do marriage right are established for our protection and benefit. When followed, they will keep the honeymoon alive as life marches on. The honeymoon doesn't have to end when the boat docks, the plane lands, or the young bride is carried over the threshold. The honeymoon, in God's plan, is the attainable goal of living side by side with a God-given spouse in a permanent relationship that makes both people better than they would be alone. It should be the long-term atmosphere of the marriage relationship, not a fleeting few months of enjoyment that are then lost forever. So let's look at this honeymoon life that we can build with our spouse.

The honeymoon as we know it actually has a rather interesting background. There are two predominant beliefs concerning its origin. Some say the term *honeymoon* is Nordic and was used to describe the act of a man who raided a neighboring village and took a woman as his wife. The man and the woman then hid from the searching relatives until either the searchers gave up, or the woman became pregnant. At that time, the man would emerge from hiding with his captured bride. From this, we get the idea that a honeymoon means a time of hiding from the rest of the world.

Others have stated a more recent origin stemming from a bride and groom drinking a wine-and-honey mixture called mead for the first thirty days of their marriage, which is one complete cycle of the moon. Thus the word *honeymoon* evolved from this practice.

I like both those stories, but even better is what the Bible says about the honeymoon. Yes, the Bible talks about the honeymoon, though it does not use the actual word. Deuteronomy 24:5 says, "A newly married man must not be drafted into the army or be given any other official responsibilities. He must be free to spend one year at home, bringing happiness to the wife he has married." Obviously, it is important to God for a man and a woman to get off to a good start in their marriage. Just as surely, He desires this special set-apart time to be the springboard to a loving and lasting relationship. So let's get started and see how this is possible.

Everything We Need for Life and Godliness

The first part of 2 Peter 1:3 tells us, "By his divine power, God has given us everything we need for living a godly life." This is the *how* and the *what* of God's plan for life and marriage. He gives us the *how* first, "By his divine power," and follows with the *what*, "everything we need for living a godly life."

And this includes living happily even after the initial stages of marriage.

The second part of the verse continues, "We have received all of this by coming to know him, the one who called us to himself by means of his marvelous glory and excellence." When we know Christ, we have everything we need to live a godly life in our home and in our marriage. That means we can live godly even after we discover that our beloved has morning breath and "bed head," and, yes, even if our spouse has the toilet-paper roll going in the wrong direction! Whether we face a minor irritation or a major impasse, God has given us everything we need to handle it in a godly way.

So how do we keep the fire burning in our marriage, and what are the spiritual instructions that can help us? Well, dear friends, as Ben Franklin once said, "Before marrying someone, keep your eyes wide open, but after marriage, keep them half shut."

There's a great deal of truth in that statement, and Scripture takes it further: "Be devoted to one another in brotherly love; give preference to one another in honor; not lagging behind in diligence, fervent in spirit, serving the Lord; rejoicing in hope, persevering in tribulation, devoted to prayer, contributing to the needs of the saints, practicing hospitality" (Rom. 12:10-13, NASB).

People who know me well know I have a thing for punctuality. Early in my marriage, it became obvious to me that my beautiful bride did not inherit that gene. So, as most men might do, I paced and grumbled and tried hard to keep my cool. My wife and I had multiple discussions about this, and I eventually decided I would correct the problem by telling my bride what time we had to be somewhere. Nothing changed.

Then I realized she didn't know how long it took to get to where we were going, so I adapted my strategy and began telling her what time we had to leave. Little did I know, however, that our definitions of "leaving" were different. To her, it meant moving toward the car and making a last-minute stop before heading to the garage. So I adopted yet another strategy.

This time I told her what time we needed to be in the car, only to learn that the vanity mirror in the bathroom was apparently insufficient for applying lip liner, because this process now had to take place in the visor mirror as we sat in the driveway. Finally, I arrived at a workable solution. I now say, "We have to be backing out of the driveway at such and such a time," and now she is always on time. (*Always* is a relative term in this application.)

What were my other options? Only to mumble and grumble and make us both miserable everywhere we went.

On the other side of that coin, I am about as flexible as an iron rod when it comes to schedule adaptations. If I didn't plan for it, it ain't gonna happen. My wife has patiently tolerated my inflexibility, and because of her, I am generally more spontaneous than I used to be. (*Generally* is a relative term in this application.)

These examples are what being "devoted to one another in brotherly love" and giving "preference to one another in honor" looks like in a marriage. If we followed that one scripture alone, it would take care of a large percentage of our problems, wouldn't it?

But therein lies the problem. Most of us do those things while we're courting our beloved but lag once the marriage ceremony has been performed. In those thrilling days of courtship, our devotion is unquestioned, we acquiesce to our beloved's desires, and we pursue our future spouse with diligence and fervor. Though our mate-to-be has defects, our love seems to cover them all. We forgive readily and find it easy to be kind and merciful. Bearing with our beloved's flaws is just an opportunity to show grace. If we could maintain this pattern of unconditional love throughout the years of our marriage, the honeymoon would indeed never end.

Listen, friends, if you want the honeymoon to never end, you must first understand something:

Personal holiness is the greatest asset of any marriage.

What that means is the more you adopt godly attributes, the more you will please your spouse. There is some truth in the oft-repeated adage among men of "happy wife, happy life." Of course, that applies for women too. Happy husbands make for happy homes as well. Whether male or female, the more you grow in personal godliness, the more harmonious your relationship with your spouse. As you mature in personal holiness, your ability to love your spouse increases, and the demands of your own flesh decrease. Take a moment and examine your life: Is your Christian behavior conditional, depending on the actions of others? Do you love only those who love you in return, or do you offer mercy, grace, and honor even to those who don't seem to deserve it? Are you living out the mandate of Romans 12:10-13, or have you discarded it as irrelevant to your married life?

Never forget, the behavior that initially won over your mate is why your spouse married you in the first place. It's who they thought you were. I have often said if your behavior now is different from your behavior when courting, you need to change it back (unless it has improved, of course). Your behavior in your home should be as exemplary as your behavior outside of the home. When your spouse fails you in some way, for example, the same patience you show to coworkers and casual acquaintances should most certainly be demonstrated to your mate.

Sadly, that is often not the case. As the honeymoon behavior begins to wane, tender mercies, kindness, and humility are often the first things to fly out the window. But this is not what the Word of God tells us to do. As Romans 12:3 exhorts, "Don't think you are better than you really are. Be honest in your evaluation of yourselves, measuring yourselves by the faith God has given us."

Isn't it interesting that the very one we spent so much time pursuing, the beloved who could do no wrong in our eyes, suddenly transforms into a person who can do nothing right after only a few short months of marriage? I want you to know today that changes in your mate's behavior are not what you need to keep the honeymoon fire burning. No, if you want that fire to burn bright, then you will have to learn to show the same godly behavior to your spouse that you so easily extend to others. Again, if your courting behavior was more tender, forgiving, and patient than is your married behavior, change it back! Go back to the things you did in the beginning, and cultivate the thoughts and ideas you practiced without effort in the early days.

Many couples cite irreconcilable differences as their reason for ending a marriage, but the truth is, every couple has them. Men and women are different by divine design, and these differences are what brings balance into the relationship. Two people don't have to agree on everything all of the time in order for their marriage to be what it ought to be. But when the two agree on and commit to living by godly behavior and practices, then the honeymoon fire will continue to blaze.

The most basic command from Scripture regarding husband-and-wife relationships is found in Ephesians 5:22–25. Though we looked at it in the previous chapter, let's read it again:

> For wives, this means submit to your husbands as to the Lord. For a husband is the head of his wife as Christ is the head of the church. He is the Savior of his body, the church. As the church submits to Christ, so you wives should submit to your husbands in everything.
> For husbands, this means love your wives, just as Christ loved the church. He gave up his life for her.

I know just what some of you husbands are saying: "Lord, I know You want me to love my wife as You love the church, but You've never met my wife!" And some of you wives are protesting, "I know I ought to submit to my husband, Lord, but he just isn't the man he's supposed to be." What do you do when you feel that way? Do you continue to complain and insist on justifying your behavior, or do you do as Colossians 3:12-13 says to do: "Clothe yourselves with tenderhearted mercy, kindness, humility, gentleness, and patience. Make allowance for each other's faults, and forgive anyone who offends you"?

The development of personal godliness is the single greatest contribution you can make to your marriage, even if your mate is not a believer.

Let me point out an important application to this passage from Ephesians before moving on. The part that tells wives to submit to their husbands as to the Lord has been misused and abused by more than one man, to be sure. Some have twisted this verse to tell wives they must submit to whatever their husbands say because the submission itself is what is fitting to the Lord. However, in reality the verse is urging wives to submit to their husbands *in* what is fitting to the Lord. In other words, wives are to submit to their husbands in those things that are acceptable to the Lord. That means, ladies, that you do not have to submit to a man's wish to bring pornography into the home, saying it will enhance your marriage. That is perversion and not fitting to the Lord. Similarly, you do not have to submit yourself to a man's habitual drunkenness or physical or verbal abuse. The basic Christian principle of "we must obey God rather than any human authority" (Acts 5:29) applies. On the other hand, ladies, if you are refusing to submit, make sure that what your husband is asking of you is not fitting to the Lord and not just something you don't want to do.

The Importance of Words

Colossians 3:16-17 holds an important truth: "Let the message about Christ, in all its richness, fill your lives. *Teach and counsel each other* with all the wisdom he gives. Sing psalms and hymns and spiritual songs to God with thankful hearts. And whatever you do or say, do it as a representative of the Lord Jesus, giving thanks through him to God the Father" (emphasis added). Couples are to teach and counsel each other in the context of their marriage. They should be learning from each other and growing in the grace of God together. After all, they're on the same team, made one by the vows exchanged in the presence of God and others.

That, I know, is easier said than done. Too often our tongues get us into trouble. There is a story that illustrates this point perfectly:

A man with six children was proud of his "achievement" and developed the habit of referring to his wife as "mother of six." Much to his wife's chagrin, he never called her "honey," "sweetheart," or "darling," even when they were out in public. One night at a dinner party, when it was time to leave, the man called loudly to his wife, "It is time to go home, mother of six," to which his exasperated bride answered, "Whenever you're ready, father of four."

Yes, "the tongue is a fire, the very world of iniquity . . . and sets on fire the course of our life" (James 3:6, NASB). Who among us has never had poorly chosen words get away from us? Unfortunately, we all do that from time to time. As

Scripture warns us, "The tongue can bring death or life; those who love to talk will reap the consequences" (Prov. 18:21). That is key to the marriage relationship. With your tongue, you can bless or curse your spouse, build up or tear down, encourage or discourage. Its power is remarkable and even frightening. Never forget this sober truth about your words:

What you say to and about your mate will soon become what is believed.

Repeated often enough, words become truth to not only the one who speaks them, but also to those who hear them. Do you remember the early days of your marriage, how sweetly you and your spouse spoke to each other? If you're like many other couples, you probably developed a pet name just for your own use. Maybe you started calling each other "honey" or "baby," or maybe you were more creative and came up with something gooey, like "sugar bunny" or "snookie-poo." The term chosen really doesn't matter. The point is, it is a term of endearment exclusive to your spouse. When spoken, it evokes feelings of warmth and belonging.

Unfortunately and far too often, those warm, fuzzy feelings fade, and before long, "sugar bunny" has become the "old lady," and "snookie-poo" is the "good-for-nothing loafer." With the change in words comes a shift of perspective. What we say is vitally important to the long-term health and stability of our marriage.

Think about it this way: When your spouse is going to meet your coworkers for the first time, they should be expecting to meet someone special because of the words you have spoken about him or her. But men, if you constantly talk about the "old ball and chain," what do you expect your fellow workers to see when they finally meet your wife? Or ladies, what will your friends see when they meet the "couch potato" for the first time? It won't be a knight in shining armor, will it?

The words that husband and wife speak to each other in their home become a self-fulfilling prophecy. Call someone a ball and chain often enough and that's exactly what they'll soon seem like to you — and maybe even to them too. Call your spouse "love of my life" and soon enough that's what they'll be in your eyes and theirs too. You see, your words determine your perspective. Ask yourself today, "Am I speaking life, or am I speaking death into my marriage?"

If you've fallen into the habit of speaking to or about your spouse in a derogatory way (even in "fun"), change that pattern today. As Philippians 4:8 instructs us, "And now, dear brothers and sisters, one final thing. Fix your thoughts on what is true, and honorable, and right, and pure, and lovely, and admirable. Think about things that are excellent and worthy of praise." How can you do this? Well, for starters, men, have you ever considered that the "old ball and chain" has kept you from wandering outside of God's will? That's an admirable thought worthy of giving God praise. Ladies, are you aware that the "couch potato" is at least parked on your couch and not on a barstool somewhere? That is a true thought to defuse resentment that builds when your husband doesn't measure up to your expectations.

Men and women of God, you will see in your spouse what your tongue has spoken about them. Put on the bond of perfection, which is love, and your marriage can be a great marriage. There are enough difficulties brought on by life without creating more by speaking silly or disrespectful words over your spouse. Remember what Proverbs 11:29 admonishes: "He who troubles his own house will inherit wind, and the foolish will be servant to the wisehearted" (NASB).

All this also holds true for singles who are dating. The man or woman who is critical of others when with you will likely become critical to others about you should you someday say "I do." Keep that in mind. If you want to test the possibility of change, then speak an encouraging word to them and see how they respond. If they change, there is hope; if not, you may be dealing with someone who struggles with pride or with an unteachable spirit. Remember, none of us are perfect, but don't settle for a *project* when you should be waiting for a *product*. If ungodly behavior is part of a person's makeup now, it is unlikely to improve after marriage. To be sure, we all grow in our relationship with the Lord, but when contemplating marriage, you should have an expectation of basic Christian behavior now, not the hope that it will develop later.

It Takes Two

Amos 3:3 asks, "Can two people walk together without agreeing on the direction?" The only way to extract all the benefits of God's plan for your marriage is for both you and your spouse to fully embrace it. That's the starting point. But it also requires you to accept not only your role in the relationship, but also your spouse's. It requires both husband and wife to look to the needs of the other and to reach out in ways that enhance love and strengthen the marriage. Men, have you ever considered that sometimes your wife may indeed feel like a ball and chain, but you are the one who can unlock the chain and treat her to a time free of duty and obligation? Ladies, maybe your couch potato is longing for you to sit next to him every once in a while. If both men and women attempt to live their roles in marriage as unto the Lord, the honeymoon will stay alive, and "happily even after" becomes an attainable goal.

Here's an important point to remember: just because one mate does not fulfill their role in the marriage, that doesn't give the other mate the right to forfeit their role. This would seem obvious, but by and large, it is a much-needed principle often neglected today. Wives should submit to their husbands, not because they deserve it, but because God has called them to do so. Husbands should love their wives as Christ loves the church, not because their wives obediently submit to them, but because God has called them to do so unconditionally. Those married to nonbelievers especially need to recognize this truth. The plan of God is always perfect, even if you are the only one following it.

Though the plan of God is perfect, the people trying to live it are not. We all bring shortfalls and liabilities into marriage, and we all need to learn from our mates. But that is dependent upon our acceptance of our God-given roles. A man will not learn how to lead from a wife who tries to do it for him, but he will learn from her sincere submission. In turn, a wife will not see the beauty in submission by being ordered to submit, but she will learn its joy through the leadership of a man who loves her as Christ loves the church.

One of the most common complaints I hear from married women is that their husbands are not the spiritual leaders in their homes. If that's the case in your home, ladies, start treating your husband as the leader, and just watch what happens. Ask him questions, and seek his opinions. If you don't ask him questions because you think he will not have the answers, then you need to know something about men. Most men hate to admit they don't know something, as evidenced by their unwillingness to ask for directions. If a woman asks her husband a spiritual question, she honors his position as head of the home and encourages him to seek the answers to spiritual questions. To a certain degree, this even applies to those women married to nonbelievers. If that is you, I encourage you to make your mate a part of your spiritual life, as much as he will allow it, and watch what happens over time. You'll be surprised!

Men often complain that their wives refuse to submit to them, but quoting "wives, submit to your husbands" will not make them submit. The way for men to encourage willing submission is to protect their wives from the spots and wrinkles all too prevalent in the world. Remember, men, your wife did not marry another father and does not want to be dealt with as though she is still a child. She is your helpmate, and according to God, she is comparable to you. Her role is only different, not less.

The word *head* used in Ephesians 5:23 means "the part most readily taken hold of." Let me put it like this: men, when your home is out of order, it's your noggin that God will come knocking on first! You set the climate for the home, not as a king over his subjects, but as a loving covering for your bride. Treat your wife like Jesus does the church, and she will become as precious in your eyes as the church is to Jesus.

Friends, we also need to be careful of drawing our understanding of home and family from the media. Shows like *Modern Family* might be what some families look like today, but society does not define marriage. God does, and He does not change. Nor do our marriages have to be full of the bickering and sarcasm of the most famous honeymooners of all, Ralph and Alice Kramden of TV fame (I'm dating myself here). There is a plan—God's plan—to follow, and when we deviate from it, we move away from all the blessings that go with it. Be a godly man or woman and practice the basic Christian principles in your marriage. Speak life, not death, into your marriage, for what comes from your mouth will soon be manifested in what you see. Nothing good, noble, or pure will be visible to you if you persist in allowing the words of your tongue to destroy your perspective of your spouse. Use the tongue for praise and exhortation, thanking God for His plan and your spouse, and watch your perspective change even if actual behavior remains the same.

All of us fail, both in marriage and in other areas of life. In those times, we need to remember the words of Scripture: "Get rid of all bitterness, rage, anger, harsh words, and slander, as well as all types of evil behavior. Instead, be kind to each other, tenderhearted, forgiving one another, just as God through Christ has forgiven you" (Eph. 4:31–32). It is a sure thing that your spouse will offend you, intentionally or unintentionally. In those times, respond by giving grace. Isn't this what you ask of God when you fail Him? Shouldn't marriage be the first place that the manifestation of God's grace is seen? What better place than marriage to seek to be like God Himself!

Again, all of us are fallible human beings, and we all bring defects into marriage. But marriage is as much about making accommodations for the limitations of others as it is about changing our own shortcomings. Remember, reacting in sin to something about your mate that you don't like is never the answer to a marriage problem. Choose instead to honor your mate as though Christ's transformational power had already done its work in them, and you will see it eventually become a reality.

Is the honeymoon over in your marriage, dear friend? It doesn't have to be, for that's not how God designed it. I urge you today to do marriage right! Do the things you did at the beginning, and watch the flame of love rekindle. Become again the mate your spouse fell in love with in the first place. Sincerely commit to living your marriage God's way, and watch "happily even after" become a reality!

Questions for Discussion

Principle

The honeymoon doesn't have to end. The covenant principles that allow us to do marriage right are established for our protection and benefit. When permitted, they will keep the honeymoon alive as life marches on.

Personal

Merely agreeing with God that marriage is a holy covenant does not mean we automatically know how to act in it in the most life-affirming way.

Romans 12:10–13 says, "Be devoted to one another in brotherly love; give preference to one another in honor; not lagging behind in diligence, fervent in spirit, serving the Lord; rejoicing in hope, persevering in tribulation, devoted to prayer, contributing to the needs of the saints, practicing hospitality" (NASB).

- Break this passage into its individual parts, and discuss how each section, if applied in married life, would help a couple to live as perpetual honeymooners.

Read Ephesians 5:22–25.

- Discuss the different spiritual roles that men and women play in marriage.

- What are the physical and emotional differences between men and women that are meant to be a blessing but sometimes present difficulties in the marriage relationship?

Why are the words you speak about your spouse so important, both to you and to your mate?

- Give an example of a time when you used your words wisely and another example of when you used them unwisely. What happened in each scenario, and what did you learn?

How can singles tell if the person they are dating is more of a *project* or a *product*?

- Why is it dangerous to marry someone that you think will change for the better?

- Do you know someone who did this? What happened?

Purposeful

Think about the spiritual role you play in your marriage. If it differs from God's Word, identify those areas and then ask for His help in changing your heart and mind. Keep a journal, if helpful.

Sometimes we can speak to and treat people at the office, or even strangers, better than we do our own spouses.

- Practice thinking before you speak. Choose to speak life-affirming words over your spouse.

- Stop negative circular thoughts, and replace them with whatever is lovely, pure, and kind.

- Knowing that personal holiness will help your marriage grow, identify the area that you most need to work on. Write it down, and begin making the appropriate changes.

Prayer

Dear heavenly Father, I thank You that You have a plan to keep the fire burning in my marriage. Pour into my heart a passion for a successful marriage. Help the desires of my heart be Yours. Reveal to me where I need to change my thoughts, words, and actions, and then strengthen me to make those changes. Let my lips be those that praise You, and may my life be one that glorifies You. I ask You to give me a heart intent on doing my marriage right, knowing that my personal holiness matters to You and to my marriage. Please, Lord, let my marriage remain a honeymoon — period. In Jesus' name I pray. Amen.

Chapter 3

DO YOU HEAR WHAT I HEAR?

May the words of my mouth and the meditation of my heart be pleasing to you, O LORD, my rock and my redeemer.
—PSALM 19:14

How easy it is for a person to say one thing and another person to hear something completely different! That is true in all relationships, but perhaps even more so in marriage.

I cannot stress enough the importance of recognizing the genetic differences between male and female beyond the obvious physical ones. This is especially true in the realm of communication. Men and women think differently and therefore communicate differently. In a marriage, failure to recognize this often leads to misunderstanding, hurt feelings, and even divorce. So in our quest to live happily even after, we again have to take the time to examine what the Word of God says about this important topic and how to weave it into the fabric of our married life.

First Corinthians 15:33 is a good place to start. In the King James Version of the Bible, this verse reads, "Evil communications corrupts good manners." The New King James phrases it somewhat differently: "Evil company corrupts good habits." The word translated "communications" in the King James and "company" in the New King James is the Greek word *homilia,* from which we get the English word *homily*. So Paul was obviously referring to verbal communication and the way it affects others.

The biblical principle of 1 Corinthians 15:33 is undeniably true: evil (poor) communication negatively impacts manners, habits, and attitudes. I am sure we have all experienced a conversation that has degraded into rude name-calling or false accusations. But the reality is, once the words have escaped our mouths, it is impossible to call them back. It is imperative, therefore, that we learn how to speak in a way that promotes intimacy within our marriage and propels us along the path of becoming one.

Scripture is full of warnings about the danger of inappropriate, uncontrolled communication. One of my favorite passages on this topic is James 3:8-12:

> No one can tame the tongue. It is restless and evil, full of deadly poison. Sometimes it praises our Lord and Father, and sometimes it curses those who have been made in the image of God. And so blessing and cursing come pouring out of the same mouth. Surely, my brothers and sisters, this is not right! Does a spring of water bubble out with both fresh water and bitter water? Does a fig tree produce olives, or a grapevine

produce figs? No, and you can't draw fresh water from a salty spring.

To say the tongue is "restless and evil" is one of the greatest understatements of Scripture, and most of us have figured that out in our own lives by now. Even when we don't want to say certain things, they have a way of coming out of our mouths anyway. But the good news is, God can tame our tongues! He can change our bitter words to sweet and replace our salty words with fresh ones. And we have the privilege of cooperating with Him in this venture and thus transforming the atmosphere of our marriage.

Male-Female Differences in Communication

In the previous chapters, we went back to the beginning in Scripture to take a look at the covenant of marriage and God's plan for it as a lasting honeymoon. Let's go back to the beginning again and see what we can learn about communication. Genesis 2:21–22 says, "So the LORD God caused the man to fall into a deep sleep. While the man slept, the LORD God took out one of the man's ribs and closed up the opening. Then the LORD God made a woman from the rib, and he brought her to the man." God took something from Adam and used it to fashion Eve. She was literally flesh of his flesh and bone of his bone, and the powerful intimacy that was to characterize the male-female relationship was firmly established.

As we learned in chapter 2, irreconcilable differences is not a reason for divorce. Every couple has them, and it all begins with the fact that one of them is a woman and one of them is a man. That's right, the two people in a marriage are very different, and God Himself created them that way. They look different and they think different, but these differences are meant to enhance the marriage relationship, not hinder it. Yet far too often genetic differences are ignored, and the marriage is negatively impacted. More often than not, the common source is poor communication.

There is a story of an English professor who wrote the words "A woman without her man is nothing" on the board and directed the students to punctuate correctly. The men wrote, "A woman, without her man, is nothing." The women, however, wrote, "A woman: without her, man is nothing." The choice of punctuation yielded two entirely different results with very different meanings. That's how it is with our communication. Our choice of words and tone of voice can convey very different meanings to those around us.

I have personally noticed something about the different way that men and women communicate. When approaching a group of women, I have observed that though they all seem to be talking at the same time, they all seem to know what the others are saying. But men in a group talk one by one, and the others listen. Why is that? Well, I believe God purposely designed men and women to communicate differently. Men as a whole reflect Ecclesiastes 5:2: "Don't make rash promises, and don't be hasty in bringing matters before God. After all, God is in heaven, and you are here on earth. So let your words be few." Men tend to guard their words and use them sparingly. You've heard the descriptive phrase "a man of few words," haven't you? That is indeed true of many men. So ladies, if you fell in love with the strong, silent type, don't expect him to turn into "chatty Kathy" after you say "I do."

On the flip side, men, God front-loaded your bride with more words than you, and she is going to use them. If you'll listen to her, she will teach you how to communicate with her. Women as a whole tend to speak more words than men and in greater detail. I believe there is a divine reason for that. Titus 2:3–5 says, "Teach the older women to live in a way that honors God. They must not slander others or be heavy drinkers. Instead, they should teach others what is good. These older women must train the younger women to love their husbands and their children, to live wisely and be pure, to work in their homes, to do good, and to be submissive to their husbands. Then they will not bring shame on the word of God." Look at all the things women have to teach! By design, they naturally use, and even need, more words to fulfill God's plan for them.

These are generalizations, of course, but by and large, men tend to be bottom-line communicators, while women are more detail oriented. Both are valid forms of communication, and both are needed at different times, but we can all grow in our ability to express ourselves in a clear and life-affirming manner. That leads right into the first major point of this chapter:

Proper marital communication is learned behavior.

Ladies, expecting your husband to know what you need or want without you telling him is not an acceptable means of communication. It does no good to pout, "You should know what I want without me having to tell you," and it is grossly unfair to your husband. He really doesn't know what you want unless you tell him, because that's the way God designed him—analytical, logical, bottom-line. God took the details of communication and put them into woman because she would be the nurturing teacher. When He formed Eve from Adam's rib, He removed certain things and used them to form woman. To expect your husband to automatically know what you need flies in the face of the truth of creation. Your husband does not have your genetic communication code, just as you do not have his.

Let's turn to the men now. God expects men to maintain the honeymoon atmosphere in the home. That means, men, you cannot talk to your wife like she is one of the guys, neither in frequency nor quantity. Your best male buddy may be perfectly content with one-word answers and grunts of agreement, but that will never do with your wife. She is not made that way. Her genetic code predisposes her to need detailed communication that builds closeness and intimacy.

If both men and women could understand that they are genetically wired differently, a lot of problems and misunderstandings could be averted. Ladies, I want to let you into a man's brain for a minute. It is entirely possible for your husband to be madly in love with you and to have a heart and mind that longs for you all day, but to come home in the evening and never say a word about it. For him, to think and feel that way is what is important, not the verbal expression of the thoughts and feelings. I'm not trying to absolve men of the need to learn how to communicate these kinds of thoughts and feelings; I'm just trying to point out to the ladies the mind-set of the man.

The role of a man in life and in the home requires the ability to react to situations without a display of emotion. Men, by design, need to be less emotional in order to be the covering they are called to be. Many times this serves them well, but it can also be a source of contention in the home. When men do not verbalize their love for their wives, the wives are left feeling unloved and unwanted, even though that is not what is going on in their husbands' hearts. So men must learn to make the effort to speak to their wives in a way that reveals their inner thoughts and feelings.

There is a natural distinction between man-versus-woman style of communication. That is God's way of equipping each for the fulfilling of their roles. That is to be understood and accepted, but not used as an excuse to avoid growing in effective communication. So for now, ladies, just remember that your husband cannot know what you need without you helping him along. And men, thinking loving thoughts about your wife without verbally expressing them to her does not satisfy her needs. If you will learn this now, you will save yourself a world of discouragement.

Quick to Hear, But Slow to Speak

It's amazing how adaptable people are. Many men and women successfully change jobs or even careers, move to other states or countries, take up new hobbies and projects, or engage in some other form of adaptation in their lives. Yet the same people can be married for decades and never learn how to communicate with their spouses. Here is an important key that helps explain why that happens:

*Husbands and wives must learn to speak how
the other person listens.*

Let me explain what I mean. I am by nature a very passionate person, and one of the first places this manifests itself is in my communication. To this day, my wife will sometimes say to me while we are having a conversation, "Why are you getting so loud? Are you mad?" It used to make me mad when she would ask if I was mad, but it didn't matter what I thought. Our conversation was over because she doesn't listen that way.

If it seems like you and your spouse are speaking two different languages, you are: "man-ish" and woman-ish"! Each must learn how to speak in the way that the other listens. Many of us are familiar with the term *selective hearing*. This is a finely tuned craft developed by male veterans of marriage. Actually, ladies, your husbands seem to tune you out because they are bottom-line communicators. Yes, they need to use more words with you than they do with the guys, but you also have to be sensitive to their bottom-line style of communication.

We'll discuss the topic of handling conflict in a later chapter, but it's worth taking a brief stop there now. James 1:19–20 tells us, "Let every man be swift to hear, slow to speak, slow to wrath; for the wrath of man does not produce the righteousness of God" (NKJV). The Greek word for "swift" is *tachus*, which can also be translated "ready." God has given us two ears and one mouth. Could it be that we should be twice as ready to listen as we are to speak? I think that's a good assumption. Most of us, however, tend to be more ready to speak than we are to listen. And even when we do listen, we hear only those things we want to hear, like "It's time for dinner" versus "It's time to take out the trash." (There's that selective-hearing thing!)

Men, if your wife says, "You never listen to me," is she telling the truth? It is highly likely that she is, and you need to honor the way God has designed her and listen to her. Ladies, as we said a moment ago, guys are masters at checking out in the middle of the conversation, but instead of getting mad at your husband, tell him how important the subject is to you, and ask him to please listen for a moment. You'll catch a lot more flies with honey than with vinegar. (If you don't know what that means, ask someone who's been happily married a while!)

In Psalm 81:13-14, God said, "Oh, that my people would listen to me! Oh, that Israel would follow me, walking in my paths! How quickly I would then subdue their enemies! How soon my hands would be upon their foes!" Obviously, great power is released when we heed the voice of the Lord. He wants us to grasp this great truth. In a similar way, I believe, a couple who truly learns the art of listening unleashes a powerful force that ripples out from their home like a pebble cast into a pond.

Too often, however, we ignore the importance of listening to our spouse. When our mate is speaking, we use the time to prepare our rebuttal instead of stilling our heart to listen and understand what our spouse is trying to communicate. Effective communication is learned behavior, so with a little effort, we can learn the priority of being quick to hear but slow to speak. Along that line is another important communication tip for you to remember:

Nothing is ever learned while you are speaking.

There is a Spanish proverb that says two great talkers will not travel far together. Why is that true? Because half of communication is listening. Have you ever seen people in a verbal altercation who are simply trying to outtalk each other? They look pretty silly, don't they? But it's more than silly in the home—it's ugly and even damaging. For you who are just starting out in marriage, like the other things we have mentioned along the way, master this and you'll save yourself a lot of strife.

Have you ever noticed how you can't hear anything when you yawn? There is a bit of a lesson there to recognize: mouth open, ears shut. If the goal of communication is to learn what pleases your mate and how he or she listens, then it will be hard for you to learn those things if you're always the keynote speaker in your home.

I want to bring in some balance here lest you come away with the wrong idea. You are who God has made you, and there is room for your personality type in His kingdom. If we look the apostles as a collective group, we will find among them the quick-to-speak Peter as well as his quiet, consistent brother Andrew. Jesus chose them both, so He obviously saw value in both styles and accepted both. Be who you are and let your spouse be who God created them to be, but both of you learn from each other.

I think this point is best illustrated by the story of a young girl approaching her wedding day who was notorious for letting her nerves get the best of her. As the day of the wedding rehearsal arrived, she expressed her concerns to the wedding coordinator, who shared her usual counsel for nervous brides. She advised the young woman, "When you come to the back of the church, just focus on one thing at a time. Remember, walk to the end of aisle, past the altar, and to your soon-to-be husband."

The next day, as the nervous young bride walked down the aisle, the weddings guests heard her repeating to herself as she passed by, "Aisle, altar, him . . . aisle, altar, him . . ." ("I'll alter him!") Yes, there are adaptations to be made in every marriage, but the goal of one is not to alter the other.

Proverbs 1:5 says, "Let the wise listen and add to their learning, and let the discerning get guidance" (NIV). If you're wise, you will listen to your spouse, and from that listening you will learn. As you seek to communicate in your marriage, never forget the listening portion. The goal of communication is to understand, not to get your point across.

Do You Hear What I Hear?

Good communication also includes learning the effect of the words that you choose when talking with your spouse. Do they hear what you hear? Are they drawing the same conclusion as you, or do your words or the tone of your voice convey an unintended message? Listen carefully for feedback from your spouse. Don't be distressed if your mate seems to have missed your point entirely. Remember, what is perceived is what was communicated, no matter what you think you said. Go back to the drawing board and try again. Listen carefully to your mate's perception of your words, and rephrase your comments to more accurately reflect your meaning. You may have to do this several times, but remember, you are sharpening your communication skills in the process. You are showing your spouse that you are willing to listen and to invest the time that it takes to communicate effectively.

When making efforts in the arena of communication, be mindful that the male-female differences are always going to be there. Both parties are going to have to accept that concessions will have to be made, to a degree. Personally, though passionate in my communication style, I am also a bit of a quiet ponderer. Small talk is very difficult for me. I have had to learn, though, that my quietness can be perceived as indifference, so I have to make constant efforts to get outside the box of my own communication style, including at home. Nonetheless, I will always be who I am. I know that, and my wife knows that. There is a happy medium for all to arrive at in male-female communication.

Choosing Wholesome Words

I love Ephesians 4:29: "Let no unwholesome word proceed from your mouth, but only such a word as is good for edification according to the need of the moment, so that it will give grace to those who hear" (NASB). Could you imagine our world if everybody lived by this principle? A pipe dream, maybe, so let's scale it back to our marriages and our homes. Would adopting this as a practice change the atmosphere in our homes? Most certainly!

Edification is actually an architectural term that simply means "to build up." Applying that to marriage, we could say to speak only those things that build up your mate and your marriage. To borrow a colloquialism from our day, how you doing with that? The purpose of communication is clearly revealed here in Ephesians: to edify or build up so as to impart grace to the hearers. A lofty goal indeed—and we all fall short. But it is an excellent guide to help us discern what we should say and what we should not say.

Notice the first two words of Ephesians 4:29: "Let no." That is a command, something we are expected to do. But it's also a choice, as evidenced by the word "let." We can "let" or "not let" corrupt words come from our mouths. By that I don't just mean profanity—though it is certainly included—but words that do not edify, impart grace, or build up. These are unwholesome choices that have no place in our relationship with our spouse.

I think we can all recognize that adopting such a tactic in our homes would force a lot more "think before you speak" into our conversations. If the conversation filter is, "Will this encourage or build up my mate? Will our relationship and therefore our home be built up by what I am about to say?" it will naturally slow down the rapid-fire and often hurtful retorts that we have all given or received. When you are having a discussion with your spouse, do not allow corrupt communication of any kind to proceed from your mouth just so you can make your point. Yes, it may feel good to let that zinger fly, but I guarantee you, you'll regret it. When tempted to say something you shouldn't, remind yourself that the choice to disregard your words is a decision to disregard God's command for communication. That raises the bar a bit, doesn't it?

A Tree Is Known by Its Fruit

Let's examine a couple more pivotal passages in our discussion of communication. First, Proverbs 12:18 says, "The words of the reckless pierce like swords, but the tongue of the wise brings healing" (NIV). And Matthew 12:33-35 reads: "A tree is identified by its fruit. If a tree is good, its fruit will be good. If a tree is bad, its fruit will be bad. You brood of snakes! How could evil men like you speak what is good and right? For whatever is in your heart determines what you say. A good person produces good things from the treasury of a good heart, and an evil person produces evil things from the treasury of an evil heart." There is a great truth we can glean from these scriptures:

Speaking your mind is a revelation of your heart.

The condition of the heart is revealed in the words spoken. Good words come forth from a good heart, and bad words issue forth from a bad heart. It is not a question of salvation that that is in view here, but one of sanctification. You might be saved, but that doesn't mean you've been completely transformed into the image of Christ yet. Check the words you say to see just how far along you are in the sanctification process. Dear friends, have you "set apart" your words for a holy work unto God? That's what the word *sanctified* means.

There is an undeniable spiritual element to marital communication. Galatians 5:16 says, "Let the Holy Spirit guide your lives. Then you won't be doing what your sinful nature craves." There's the choice again: "Let" the Holy Spirit guide you. I don't know about you, but I suspect that I am in good and numerous company when I say I have sometimes known the right thing to do and not done it and have known the wrong thing to say and said it anyway. If you're not thinking, "Been there, done that, bought the T-shirt," then you're in a group of people so elite I've never actually met one!

Seriously, is there any part of our lives that is not to be governed by and surrendered to the Holy Spirit? I dare say the tongue, that "little member" Scripture speaks of, is a big troublemaker. It has been said that though the tongue has no bones, it is hard enough to break a heart. Let the Spirit filter the words you say and caution you against the words you should not say. Let Him crucify your flesh (which is what the tongue is also made of) and teach you how to prevent your unruly member from setting a fire that cannot be easily extinguished.

I think many married couples have a tendency to let it all hang out. Some even pride themselves on speaking their mind in their marriage relationship. Well, that might make them feel better for a moment, but you can be sure the path they leave behind is littered with hurt feelings and damaged relationships. I have often said there are two 29:11's in the Bible that every Christian needs to know. One is well known and the other sadly obscure. Jeremiah 29:11 is the one we all know, and Proverbs 29:11 is the one we all need to know: "A fool vents all his feelings, but a wise man holds them back" (NKJV). Did you happen to notice there are only two categories of communication listed here? Foolish and wise. Wise communication, again, is Spirit led and practically filtered by asking ourselves whether our words build up or tear down.

Let me make a point here to make sure you don't misunderstand. True, you should not vent any and every thought that comes to your mind, but giving your spouse the silent treatment is just as detrimental. There is a "time to be quiet and a time to speak" (Eccles. 3:7), and the wise person learns the difference.

Now, back to Matthew and the truth that our words reveal what is in our hearts. Even when times are tough in your marriage, even when your spouse has wronged you, even when you are in the right, if you use your words to tear down your spouse, it reveals more about you than it does about them. Speaking your mind no matter what, oblivious to the consequences, says something about your heart and is an indication that you have an area in your life that needs to be brought under the spiritual fruit of self-control. If you struggle in this area, do not simply default to "that's just the way I am." God is in the people-changing business, and if it is His will that our communication be a form of edification, then you and I can be sure that He will supply the power to change when we fall short in this area, just as He does in all others. I urge you to yield to Him and to allow Him to turn the bitter spring to sweet.

Proverbs 26:18–19 provides another interesting insight into communication. It reads, "Like a madman who throws firebrands, arrows and death, so is the man who deceives his neighbor, and says, 'Was I not joking?' " (NASB). We've all heard the childhood adage "sticks and stones may break my bones, but words will never hurt me." That is just not true. Words carelessly spoken in a marriage have oftentimes not been thought through and their repercussions seriously considered. I personally believe men are more prone to this than are women, but we all need to stop and think before speaking.

The verse in Proverbs warns us not to speak flippantly, claiming, "Oh, I was only joking!" How many husbands and wives do this, sarcastically flinging pointed barbs at their mates only to claim they were joking? Remember, my friend, jokes are supposed to be funny, and if your mate isn't laughing, there was no joke. More often, in fact, you're throwing a firebrand or a burning arrow with the potential of destroying your home. Instead, follow the admonition of 2 Corinthians 10:4-5: "The weapons we fight with are not the weapons of the world. On the contrary, they have divine power to demolish strongholds. We demolish arguments and every pretension that sets itself up against the knowledge of God, and we take captive every thought to make it obedient to Christ" (NIV). If you'll obey God's Word, you'll not only refrain from speaking hurtful, corrupt words, but you will also resist even the thought of them. If you don't do this, if you speak whatever is in your head, you are playing right into the devil's hand and possibly speaking thoughts that originate from him. The consequences of that can be disastrous for your marriage.

The Power of Words

There is a proverb that says the problem with someone quick to speak is that they often say things they haven't thought of yet! We need to remember that once words are spoken, their power is released. Following a cruel comment with, "Sorry, I didn't really mean it" does little to lessen the blow. Saying, "You misunderstood me" can be nothing more than an attempt to shift the blame to your spouse and denies your responsibility to learn how to speak in a way that your mate can understand. Always remember:

Words can create wounds that other words cannot heal.

As much as I hate to admit it, I once was the master of disaster when it came to this particular subject. Being a man, it was not unusual for me to trade insulting barbs with my male friends. We picked on and insulted each other with regularity. Words meant nothing; they were just that — words. Between us guys it was almost as though the one who concocted the greatest insult was king for the day. Sadly, for some time, I applied this principle at home as well, though not with the same spirit. I was one of those who did not understand that words matter and that *how* something is said can easily negate *what* is said. I am thankful for my wife's patience and the Lord's mercy in this area, as my behavior before my recommitment to the Lord was far less than exceptional. My point is, God can turn things around for anyone at any time, and a new pattern can be established. But beware, the wounds created by your words can last a long, long time.

This is not to say there will never be innocent misunderstandings and communication misfires; I am talking about a repeated pattern where words are spoken hastily or harshly, hurt feelings result, and an apology is needed. If this has been going on in your home — words spoken carelessly, flippantly, or even cruelly — there is only one course of action to take, and that is found in Proverbs 26:20: "For lack of wood the fire goes out" (NASB). Quit feeding the fire created by your ill-spoken words, and the fire will go out. Refuse to say things for effect that you assume you will be able to repair later. It doesn't work that way.

Singles, if you are dating someone who is already throwing firebrands your way and then apologizing for it, don't let the relationship go any further until the fire has been quenched. Remember, that person is on his or her best behavior while wooing you. If you marry someone like that, it seldom improves after marriage, I assure you. You will only be setting yourself up for more of the same—and probably worse.

Dear friends, make up your mind to live by Psalm 19:14: "May the words of my mouth and the meditation of my heart be pleasing to you, O LORD, my rock and my redeemer." Is the psalmist only talking about the words we speak to God, or is he talking about all words? I believe it is both. Words carry power, and using them in a way that requires constant explanation or apology is not pleasing to God. Words can wound deeply, and sometimes the wound refuses to heal, while other times the scar left behind is permanent and ugly.

The tongue has set on fire many a home, sad to say. But today we can decide in our hearts to quit putting wood on the fire and to let it go out. We can make our words like "golden apples in a silver basket" (Prov. 25:11). That's a beautiful picture, isn't it? When we adorn our marital relationship with fitly spoken words, our mate will wear them like jewels. This, dear friend, is how our communication becomes right in the eyes of God and brings blessings into our home—the blessing of communication that builds up and never tears down, the blessing of misunderstood words being the exception rather than the rule, the blessing of apology having the ability to heal because the communication pattern in the home is not one of inflicting wounds. It is how we learn to answer an unequivocal yes to the question, do you hear what I hear? If you will learn to speak how your mate listens, you will be well on your way to living happily even after all the communication breakdowns of the past.

Questions for Discussion

Principle

There are God-designed genetic differences between male and female beyond the obvious physical ones. This is especially true in the realm of communication. Men and women think differently and therefore communicate differently. Husbands and wives must learn to speak in such a manner that the other one can hear them.

Personal

How easy it is for a person to say one thing and another person to hear something completely different! That is true in all relationships, but perhaps even more so in marriage.

Have you ever had a problem with your spouse mainly because you did not understand his or her style of communication?

How would understanding the basic differences in male-female communication help you avoid problems in the future?

Have you ever known someone to excuse their poor communication skills by saying, "That's just the way I am"?

- Why is this not a valid excuse?

In marriage or dating relationships, how can we acknowledge basic male-female differences without allowing them to become excuses for wrong behavior?

What does it mean to speak in the way that another person listens?

- Give examples of this from your own life.
- Are you better at speaking or at listening?
- What could you do to grow in the weaker area?

List helpful phrases that a husband or wife could say to build each other up.

- Why do you think some people have a problem speaking uplifting, encouraging words?

What are the effects of edifying communication in a relationship?

Scripture says, "Out of the abundance of the heart the mouth speaketh" (Matt. 12:34, KJV). By now we've been seeing the direct route from the things we think in our hearts to those things that roll off our tongues. Discuss the relationship between the thoughts we harbor in our minds and hearts to the words we speak with our mouths.

- How are the two related, both for good and bad?

Purposeful

Since we know that the tongue has the incendiary ability to set our homes on fire, let's be purposeful in our hearts in making sure we do not put any more wood on that fire. Instead, let's make our words like "golden apples in a silver basket" (Prov. 25:11).

Start speaking your list of uplifting phrases to your spouse. This does not have to be done with wonderful, passionate feelings, but neither should it be spoken with a robotic intonation. It should come from a place of sincerely wanting your covenant with God and your spouse to succeed. Oftentimes emotions, passions, and feelings will follow obedience, so do the right thing regardless of feelings. Keep in mind that this is not a one-time "see if it works" deal, but rather a habit to put into daily practice.

Practice listening to your spouse rather than trying to speak over them.

- Give them the space they need to convey their own thoughts without your being punitive.

If you're reading this as a couple, exchange your lists with each other. These are not lists of demands, but rather suggestions on how you can speak to each other in a way that you will help you to hear each other better.

Prayer

Dear heavenly Father, I ask that You give me the power and wisdom of the Holy Spirit to speak life into my marriage and over my spouse. Lord, I desire to build up and not tear down. Please forgive me where I have done it wrong in the past, and help me to speak in a manner that is pleasing to You. Give me a tender heart to Your Holy Spirit. Help me be quick to listen and slow to speak. I ask You to cause what I have learned to change my soul in such a way that those closest to me are witnesses of this transformation. Wash me, and renew a right spirit within me. In Jesus' name I pray. Amen.

Chapter 4

WHAT'S LOVE GOT TO DO WITH IT?

Love never gives up, never loses faith, is always hopeful, and endures through every circumstance.

—1 CORINTHIANS 13:7

We've looked at the holy institution of marriage as a covenant between a man and a woman. We've learned that marriage is meant to be a lasting honeymoon. We've explained that poor communication is probably the most common area of marital weakness. In all this discussion, however, we've said very little about love, though love is the reason why most couples get married in the first place. Maybe Tina Turner didn't get it when she belted out, "What's love got to do with it?" but in reality love has everything to do with it—at least the kind of love that Scripture so clearly talks about.

Everybody wants love, and most of us spend a good portion of our lives looking for it. If you were to ask ten people to define love, you would probably get ten different answers. Look at how a panel of "experts" took a shot at defining love and its place in marriage:

If falling in love is anything like learning how to spell, I don't want to do it. It takes too long.

—Glenn, age 7

Love is like an avalanche where you have to run for your life.

—John, age 9

I think you're supposed to get shot with an arrow or something, but the rest of it isn't supposed to be so painful.

—Manuel, age 8

No one is sure why it happens, but I heard it has something to do with how you smell. That's why perfume and deodorant are so popular.

—Mae, age 9

It gives me a headache to think about that stuff. I don't need that kind of trouble.

—Kenny, age 7

One of you should know how to write a check. Because even if you have tons of love, there is still going to be a lot of bills.

—Ava, age 8

Here are my two personal favorites, showing the difference between the male brain and the female brain even at a young age:

Most men are brainless, so you might have to try more than once to find a live one.

—Angie, age 10

Love will find you, even if you are trying to hide from it. I've been trying to hide from it since I was five, but the girls keep finding me.

— Dave, age 8

Though we laugh at the childish responses, most of us adults would be just as hard pressed to come up with an adequate definition of love and the role it plays in marriage. So why do couples get married, or to ask again Tina Turner's question, "What's love got to do with it?" Is it really just a "secondhand emotion" as the song states, or is it something more — something deep and abiding that can be identified in Scripture and duplicated in our lives?

Let's start our discussion of scriptural love by taking a look at Ephesians 5:33: "So again I say, each man must love his wife as he loves himself, and the wife must respect her husband." Interestingly, nowhere in Scripture are wives exhorted to love their husbands, not because they're not supposed to, but because God instead emphasizes the divine order that brings the realization of fullest potential. In the home, that begins with husbands loving their wives as Christ loves the church. From that foundational premise, we can see what love has to do with marriage from three vantage points: (1) love's attributes, (2) love's allure, and (3) love's attitude.

Love's Attributes

We cannot know the role of love in marriage if we do not know what love is. Thankfully, as with every aspect of life, the

Bible has the answer. Read 1 Corinthians 13:4–8 in the New American Standard translation:

> Love is patient, love is kind and is not jealous; love does not brag and is not arrogant, does not act unbecomingly; it does not seek its own, is not provoked, does not take into account a wrong suffered, does not rejoice in unrighteousness, but rejoices with the truth; bears all things, believes all things, hopes all things, endures all things.
> Love never fails.

Look at that last sentence: love never what? Love never fails, and *never* means never. I know what some of you are thinking: "Well, that may be true most of the time, but not in my case"; or "That doesn't apply to me because my spouse is not a believer." But *never* indeed means never, and there are no exceptions. Love done God's way never fails. That is its first and primary attribute.

Look again at the passage above. You'll find no promise of goose bumps, pounding hearts, and frenzied emotions whipped to a state of ecstasy. The common descriptions of love that abound in our society are never mentioned. As the old DC Talk song reminds us, "love is a verb," and Paul, here in 1 Corinthians, uses a string of fifteen Greek verbs to define love's attributes, including what love does and does not do: ". . . does not brag . . . does not act unbecomingly . . . bears all things . . . hopes all things . . ." According to Scripture, these are the attributes of true love.

The attributes of love so clearly defined in 1 Corinthians 13 are summed up in Philippians 2:3: "Let nothing be done through selfish ambition or conceit, but in lowliness of mind let each esteem others better than himself" (NKJV). The word "esteem" is the Greek word *hegeomai*, which means "to command with official authority." This command of God, I believe, is how we can have a love in our marriage that will never fail. It is why Ephesians can command husbands to love their wives as Christ loves the church. Since love is a verb, it can be expressed at all times by the fruit of the spirit of self-control.

Love's attributes are what love does no matter how love feels. When we esteem our mate more highly than we esteem ourselves, we are making an "official" choice to love, commanding ourselves with the full authority of God to look to our mate's interests above our own. Sadly, many marriages today end or struggle because husband and wife don't understand this aspect of sacrificial love, a proactive, consistent, satisfying love that puts the needs of others first.

We live in a very me-centered society, and this is one of the greatest enemies of marriage today. Too many people are *responsive* rather than *responsible* in loving their mates. What I mean by that is love is too often performance based: "I'll love you the way you want me to, but you have to earn or deserve it first." This is not how God has defined love. "We love Him because He first loved us" (NKJV) is how 1 John 4:19 puts it. God defines love, not as feelings oriented or performance dictated, but as something extended first that the same might be received in return. Far too often in our day, however, when the intensity of emotion wanes or the routine of everyday life quenches the passion of love's fire, couples declare they are not in love anymore and look for a way out.

Listen, those of you who are married, dating, or looking for that special someone. Take note of what I'm about to say, and hide it in your heart for those moments when you question the direction or sustainability of your marriage:

Love cannot be fallen out of — only forsaken.

Remember, love never fails. When someone says they are not in love anymore, they are revealing an unwillingness to suffer long and be kind, to not envy, to think no evil of their spouse, and to bear all things. They are stating they will not believe for the best, hope in all circumstances, and endure all things. They reject practicing all those self-sacrificing actions described in 1 Corinthians 13. What they are really saying is, "I am going to disregard God's command to put my mate's needs above my own." In essence, because of their feelings, they are forsaking the attributes of true love.

I realize there are some exceptions to this, and I will address that later, but for now I want you to grasp this principle: the Christian marriage has a distinct advantage over the non-Christian marriage because of the divine power within believers to live out the attributes of love. The Christian surrendered to the Lord lives out the command of 1 John 4:7-8: "Dear friends, let us continue to love one another, for love comes from God. Anyone who loves is a child of God and knows God. But anyone who does not love does not know God, for God is love." As Christians, if we can do all things through Christ, if He has given us all things pertaining to life and godliness, if we have received every spiritual blessing in heavenly places, then there is no reason the love in our marriage should fail.

Again, if you feel like love has left your marriage, it's because you're not doing marriage right. Don't misunderstand me. I am not saying that love is a clinical set of rules that can be followed without any expectation of feelings or romance. What I am saying is that love is a series of attributes that, when embraced, creates the emotional ties and feelings that never fail. Love is not the *feelings*, but the *actions* that precipitate the feelings. That's an important point to remember. One of the main reasons that the divorce rate is as high in the church as it is in the world, I believe, is that we have reduced love to a "secondhand emotion" and a "sweet old-fashioned notion," as Tina Turner said. We have bought into the world's definition of love instead of God's. We are dependent on emotion, and when emotions change, we assume love has failed.

Love definitely includes feelings and emotions, but it is not strictly defined by them. Think about this: Have you ever gotten out of bed one morning and just didn't feel right? Did you go to work feeling mad at the world and despising your job, thinking that any other job would be better than this one? In other words, you were having an off day, and it colored your perspective. Millions of people have had these kinds of feelings and emotions one day and then felt very differently the next day, but they didn't quit their jobs when they were feeling bad. Sadly, some people do not treat their marriage, which is sacred and holy before God, with as much respect as they do their job. When they don't feel like they used to, they're out of there.

If we were to return to God's definition of love as recorded in 1 Corinthians 13, if we were to put into practice the attributes of love, what a difference that would make in our marriages! Imagine your marriage if patience, kindness, and long-suffering were the norm and not the exception. What would happen if arrogance were banished, rudeness discarded, and provocation ignored? If you think that's too tall of an order, consider again. Didn't Jesus our Savior exemplify all those attributes of love and more when He walked among us—even all the way to the cross?

Dear friends, love cannot be fallen out of, only forsaken. Before you give up on your marriage, before you allow the devil to seize control of your thought life, before you surrender without a whimper while the enemy tears asunder what God has put together, hold up the mirror of 1 Corinthians 13 to see if you have been acting in love and thus doing marriage right. That is the gauge you go by—not the world's faulty assumptions. If you fall short of the standard of God's Word, commit today to living out love's attributes, and then watch what happens!

Let me make one final comment here about love's attributes. I know some of you are asking, "My mate isn't a believer. What do I do? Does the same standard apply to me as applies to those in a Christian marriage?" Generally speaking, yes, the same standard applies. God's commands are the same for each of us. However, Scripture does recognize the unique challenge for those married to unbelievers and addresses it: "In the same way, you wives must accept the authority of your husbands. Then, even if some refuse to obey the Good News, your godly lives will speak to them without any words. They will be won over by observing your pure and reverent lives" (1 Pet. 3:1-2).

Though verse 1 says "wives," it applies, of course, to men as well. The point is, living a pure and reverent life before an unbelieving spouse, or, in other words, living out love's attributes, is an effective way to reach their soul and lead them to salvation. Your words will render only a limited effect, but your actions will speak much more loudly of your love for your spouse as well as the Savior you serve. That is the key to living with an unbeliever, and the Holy Spirit who dwells within you will help you to do even this great task.

Sometimes, however, a believer does everything possible to live peaceably and lovingly with an unbelieving spouse, but the unbeliever still rejects God's ways and plans for marriage. What then? Well, again Scripture gives the answer, and again it applies equally to either gender. First Corinthians 7:12-16 reads as follows:

> Now, I will speak to the rest of you, though I do not have a direct command from the Lord. If a Christian man has a wife who is not a believer and she is willing to continue living with him, he must not leave her. And if a Christian woman has a husband who is not a believer and he is willing to continue living with her, she must not leave him. For the Christian wife brings holiness to her marriage, and the Christian husband brings holiness to his marriage. Otherwise, your children would not be holy, but now they are holy. (But if the husband or wife who isn't a believer insists on leaving, let them

go. In such cases the Christian husband or wife is no longer bound to the other, for God has called you to live in peace.) Don't you wives realize that your husbands might be saved because of you? And don't you husbands realize that your wives might be saved because of you?

So, you see, love's attributes will generally prevail, and we are called to live them out to the best of our ability whether we think they will work or not in our particular situation. I encourage you to read again 1 Corinthians 13 in its entirety. Ask the Holy Spirit to identify the areas in which you fall short, and commit to growing in those specific attributes. When you do, you will find the secret to the unfailing love that keeps you living happily even after.

Love's Allure

What about romance and sexual intimacy? What role do they play in married life, and what are the boundaries for dating couples? Well, God has a plan here, and it is laid out in 1 Corinthians 7:1–5. I will give it to you in just a minute, but first, let's go back to our panel of experts quoted earlier in this chapter and see what they had to say about kissing, a basic part of physical intimacy:

> When a person gets kissed for the first time, they fall down, and they don't get up for at least an hour.
> —WENDY, AGE 8

Never kiss in front of other people. It's a big embarrassing thing if anybody sees you. But if nobody sees you, I might be willing to try it with a handsome boy, but just for a few hours.

—Kally, age 9

It's never okay to kiss a boy. They always slobber all over you. That's why I stopped doing it.

—Tammy, age 10

I know one reason kissing was created. It makes you feel warm all over, and they didn't always have electric heat or fireplaces or even stoves in their houses.

—Gina, age 8

The rule goes like this: if you kiss someone, then you should marry her and have kids with her. It's the right thing to do.

—Howard, age 8

Maybe Howard got it at least partially right; certain actions are reserved exclusively for marriage. Genesis 2:24 reminds us of God's original plan in male-female relationships: "This explains why a man leaves his father and mother and is *joined* to his wife, and the two are united into one" (emphasis added). God joined the man to the woman, both symbolically and physically, and from this union sexual intimacy was not only birthed but also sanctioned. Adam and Eve became one in every sense of the word, and there was no shame in it. What a beautiful picture of what sex is supposed to be!

Sexual intimacy was created by God. It is natural, it is wonderful, it is divinely sanctioned; and as with everything else God created, it is good — when used in alignment with His design and plan. But sexual intimacy can be abused and used in ways that God never intended. That is the enemy's plan, because he always perverts God's pure design into an enticing counterfeit that lures us from God's path. Sexual intimacy is like a fire. When confined to the fireplace, its proper abode, it brings warmth and comfort. If the fire escapes the fireplace, however, it becomes an enemy that consumes everything in its path. Satan knows he cannot reverse the will of God. He knows that sexual passion is a normal part of life, so his effort has been directed toward redefining the fireplace, taking what is natural and normal and expanding the boundaries God has prescribed for it.

Let me address the singles reading this book. If you profess godliness, then you must set in place ahead of time standards that will protect you from compromising moments when you are tempted to sin. Learn what the Scriptures say about sexual propriety, and make that part of your spiritual fabric. Refuse to entertain thoughts and opinions contrary to the Word of God. Your stand may not be popular, but it is indeed scriptural. Remember, it's not what we think that matters, nor should we glean our moral standards from cultural acceptability. It might be okay with society to have sex before marriage, but it's not okay with God—and that is what counts.

Ephesians 5:3-5 gives us some clear parameters in the area of sexual intimacy: "Let there be no sexual immorality, impurity, or greed among you. Such sins have no place among God's people. Obscene stories, foolish talk, and coarse jokes—these are not for you. Instead, let there be thankfulness to God. You can be sure that no immoral, impure, or greedy person will inherit the Kingdom of Christ and of God." Not only are God's people to refrain from overt sexual immorality, but they are also to have no part in obscenity, coarseness, and immorality of any kind. That's a far cry from what we see in our society, isn't it?

Let me remind you that Paul is talking about unrepentant sexual immorality and other abhorrent behaviors. God can and will forgive any sin except unconfessed sin. First John 1:9 says, "If we confess our sins, He is faithful and just to forgive us our sins and to cleanse us from all unrighteousness" (NKJV). The word *confess* means "to see or speak as the same." In other words, God requires that we see sin the way He sees it and accept His definition of it. This includes sexual sin. When we acknowledge that we are sinners, He extends His forgiveness. If we say He does not have the right to set boundaries on sexual behavior, then we are not in agreement with Him.

So many people today—even some within the church—seem to feel that anything is okay if the two people involved agree to it. If a couple agrees to live together as "friends with benefits," then whose business is that? Well, that might be true if God had not provided a moral compass to steer us, but He did, and His blessing is tied to obedience to His commands. That's seen in the sad statistic that 85 percent of those who live together before marriage end up in divorce, compared to the average 50 percent rate. Why? God does not bless sin, and living together before marriage is sin. Remember, it doesn't matter what we think.

Sexual activity, in God's eyes, is reserved for those who are married, and then only with each other. It may be in vogue to have an open marriage or extramarital sexual encounters, but again, this is outside God's boundaries of permissible sex. Furthermore, there is no place for sex in the life of the unmarried. The desire can be there, and the longing can be there—these are natural and God-ordained things—but God has limited sexual activity to the married. When an unmarried person engages in sexual relations, the Bible calls it *fornication*, and fornication is a sin. Ephesians 5:5-7 warns us, "No fornicator, unclean person, nor covetous man, who is an idolater, has any inheritance in the kingdom of Christ and God. Let no one deceive you with empty words, for because of these things the wrath of God comes upon the sons of disobedience. Therefore do not be partakers with them" (NKJV). Be not deceived, my brother and sister, no matter what the accepted norm may be, God says sex outside of marriage is sin.

I have had many dating and engaged couples ask me, "How far can we go in our physical relationship?" When I hear that question, it tells me the couple is trying to redefine the fireplace. And when you play with fire, you will most certainly be burned. You may call me old-fashioned on this, but this is the Word of God, and I'm going to side with Him. If you are single and dating and wondering where to place the boundary line in your physical relationship, let me suggest this: don't do anything in private that you wouldn't do while sitting in church. That may seem extreme to you, but remember, you are God's temple and should be treated with decorum and respect. Honor God and honor yourself by recognizing your worth in God's kingdom. Don't allow nakedness and fornication to bring shame into your life that may be very hard to get rid of. Don't do it!

Too many people today, married and unmarried, confuse lust with love. I think TV and movies have a lot to do with that. Listen, ladies, you may think the "days of our lives" were great when we were all "young and restless" and passions were "bold and beautiful." Your life may now seem confined to "dark shadows" and your marriage seem but a ward in a "general hospital." But life is not a soap opera, and you'll learn nothing of value by feeding your mind with such fruitless content. It's just one way of many to fan a sinful flame of lust by not honoring the alluring aspects of true love.

Men, the Bible warns us to never let down our guard concerning sexual purity. Job had adult children living away from home, making it likely he was a grandfather. Yet he still made a covenant with his eyes not to look lustfully after young women (Job 31:1). You and I must do the same, including fleeing from all forms of pornography.

Married men and women alike bear responsibility in dealing with their sexual passions. First Corinthians 7:5 says, "Do not deprive each other of sexual relations, unless you both agree to refrain from sexual intimacy for a limited time so you can give yourselves more completely to prayer. Afterward, you should come together again so that Satan won't be able to tempt you because of your lack of self-control." Neither the man nor the woman has exclusive rights to their own bodies, nor are they to withhold from each other except by mutual consent for a specific time of prayer. Even then, they are expected to come together again so that Satan cannot exploit the alluring aspect of married love with the perversion of lust.

Another thing to remember about love and sexual intimacy in marriage is this:

> *What God has given as a treasure is never*
> *to be used as a tactic.*

Contrary to popular opinion, human beings are not mere animals whose sexual urges are satisfied in the male conquest of the female. No, God did not create human sexuality to work like that. Men, sex is not just for you and your needs. God never intended for you to demand your rights because, after all, you are the "head of the house." And ladies, sex is not a tactical weapon that you bestow when you're pleased with your husband's behavior and withhold when he has not measured up to your arbitrary standards of conduct. Sexual intimacy in marriage is designed for the pleasure and benefit of both husband and wife. It's supposed to bring you together, not tear you apart.

Hebrews 13:4 says, "Give honor to marriage, and remain faithful to one another in marriage. God will surely judge people who are immoral and those who commit adultery." Sexual intimacy was created by God, and it is good. However, that does not mean that married couples have the right to introduce sinful behavior to allegedly enhance their relationship. That is a perversion of God's truth. In the marriage relationship, both husband and wife must look to the good of the other in the area of sexual intimacy. Men, you cannot treat your wife like garbage and then expect her to warm up to you sexually. Ladies, your body is not your own; you have a responsibility to be attentive to your husband's needs and not to wield your sexual power as a bargaining tool. Dating couples, do not take what God has ordained for marriage as your own until that man or woman has said "I do." The man who pressures a young woman by saying, "If you love me, you will sleep with me" will have no respect for her in the morning if she gives in. The man who loves a woman as God has commanded will protect his beloved's reputation and will want a bride without spot or wrinkle.

So, love's attributes are clearly defined, and love's allure must be properly contained, but what about love's attitude?

Love's Attitude

First Peter 4:8 beautifully sums up love's attitude: "Most important of all, continue to show deep love for each other, for love covers a multitude of sins." Love covers a multitude of sins—wow, that's powerful, isn't it? Let me share with you a story that shows just how powerful love's attitude can be.

I knew a man who was an abusive drunk and who tormented his wife from the opening months of their marriage. After many painful events and a final out-of-control altercation, the woman could take no more and left her husband. Following his usual pattern, the man was quite ashamed of his behavior after he sobered up, but it was too late this time. A line had been crossed, and he had gone too far. His wife was gone and with her their tiny daughter. Desperate to make amends, the man began calling friends and family in a frantic search to find his wife and child, but no one would even take his call.

Days rolled into weeks, but still his wife was nowhere to be found. Then, one day when he was at work, a uniformed officer served him with papers that announced his marriage was coming to an end. His wife wanted a divorce. Heartbroken, the man could do little more than let the natural course of events unfold. The weeks turned into months, and during that time, his little girl's second birthday came and went. He was not present for the occasion, nor had he even been invited—and rightfully so.

After eight long months of separation, the man's phone rang one day, and his wife was on the line. The conversation was brief, with his wife saying, "I just wanted to tell you that I went to church with my sister and asked Jesus into my heart." The man, a prodigal himself, said he was happy for her, and the phone call ended. Nothing had really changed, but at least he had spoken to his wife.

Several days later, in a desperate effort to reconnect with his estranged wife, the man again made the round of phone calls to family and friends in search of his wife and daughter. Much to his surprise, the call to his mother-in-law's home put him on the phone with his wife. An agreement was made to meet, and for the first time in eight months, this hateful man and his abused wife would stand face-to-face.

The day of the meeting arrived. . . . I will never forget the brown skirt and matching jacket my wife wore on that summer afternoon in 1980. . . . I will never forget the wonder in my heart as I laid eyes on my daughter and saw her transformation from baby to little girl in the course of eight long months. . . . I will never forget the joy of undeserved hope that sprang alive in my heart that day. . . . It soon became apparent that God had a plan for my wife and me *even after* our marriage had suffered great trauma. That is why I can stand before you today and shout for all to hear:

Love's greatest attitude is a willingness to forgive.

Dear friends, the summation of love's attitude has nothing to do with feelings, but everything to do with forgiveness. When we forgive, we are modeling exactly what our heavenly Father does: "O Lord, you are so good, so ready to forgive, so full of unfailing love for all who ask for your help" (Ps. 86:5). Examine yourself. Are you allowing the devil to have his way in your home? Is unforgiveness in your heart stifling love's attributes, hindering love's allure, and quenching love's attitude? It doesn't have to be that way.

Hebrews 12:14–15 gives us the solution: "Work at living in peace with everyone, and work at living a holy life, for those who are not holy will not see the Lord. Look after each other so that none of you fails to receive the grace of God. Watch out that no poisonous root of bitterness grows up to trouble you, corrupting many." Think about it. What do you love most about God? Yes, I know His omnipresence is awe inspiring. His omniscience, the fact that He knows everything, overwhelms me. And His magnificent omnipotence, His absolute and ultimate power and authority, forces me to my knees in adoration. But above all that, He is a God who loves. Before I ever loved Him, He loved me (again, 1 John 4:19), and because of that love, He was willing to forgive my sins through His Son Jesus Christ before I ever acknowledged that I wanted forgiveness.

My dear brothers and sisters in Christ, forgiveness is the ultimate attitude of love—whether it is God's love or human love we are talking about. What would God's love mean to us if it did not come with forgiveness so total and complete that it is as though we had never sinned? No, God's love is not partial, but full. It covers the multitude of human wrongs and joyously proclaims, "It is finished!" The debt is paid, and we are free to walk in God's love and forgiveness—and to extend it to others.

How can we experience the fullness of marriage without the ultimate power of love's forgiveness? I tell you, it is not possible. Husbands and wives, be the first in your marriage to be kind, patient, and long-suffering. Be the first to bear all things, to endure all things—even when you think your spouse doesn't deserve it. Be the first to love.

Romans 5:8 says, "But God showed his great love for us by sending Christ to die for us while we were still sinners." *While we were still sinners . . .* Our being deserving had nothing to do with Christ demonstrating His love for us, and it has nothing to do with demonstrating love in our marriages either. We are called to be like our Savior, and that means making the first move, loving unconditionally, forgiving without strings attached.

As I end this chapter, I'm not asking whether you are still in love with your spouse, but whether you have forsaken love because of the bitterness of unforgiveness. Maybe you feel like it's too late for you, but I tell you today, love never fails, especially when forgiveness comes into play and is both given and received. Love covers a multitude of sins, and when undeserved forgiveness is extended, we experience divine love as closely as we can in this life. And the first place we should see this kind of love in action is between two people who have said "I do."

One final word before we move on. Some of you may be thinking, "Not gonna happen, pastor. My marriage is dead. There are no feelings of love, and we both want it to end." My dear friend, there was never a marriage more dead than mine, never a marriage with less hope than mine. My wife hated me and had every right to after all I had done, but our feelings, or lack of them, did not negate God's plan. When my wife and I reconciled, she took a great risk on me, and the feelings of love did not return instantaneously. However, over time, the mechanics of love restored the feelings of love.

I want to let you in on a little secret from my marriage. Some of the terrible things I have done that I wish I could forget, my beautiful bride doesn't even remember. Because they are imbedded in my memory, I write as though these things happened recently, but her love and God's love have covered a multitude of sins. I know it's true because I have seen it with my own eyes and heard it with my own ears. My wife and I are a long way from 1980, and we are both very different people from the ones we used to be, thanks be to God. We are now in our thirty-sixth year of marriage, and I am as crazy about her as she is about me.

Rest assured, my friend, there is hope for your marriage too, and feelings can be restored for you just as they were for my wife and me. Maybe you just need to take a moment and say "I do" again to the attributes of love. Maybe you need to reignite the flame of love's allure. And just maybe you need to wrap it all up in love's attitude of forgiveness. God can heal and restore any marriage, no matter how broken. You can live happily even after with the spouse of your youth—even after unbearable pain and betrayal have stripped you of all hope. I know it's true because it happened to me. And if it happened to me, it can happen to you.

Questions for Discussion

<u>Principle</u>

Love's principal attributes are what love does no matter how love feels. When we esteem our mate more highly than we esteem ourselves, we are making an "official" choice to love, commanding ourselves with the full authority of God to look to our mate's interests above our own.

<u>Personal</u>

List as many attributes as you can think of that describe true love in a marriage.

- Why must these attributes be demonstrated in actions and not just spoken in words in order to be valid expressions of love?

In the course of your lifetime, how have you seen people's perception of love's allure (sexual intimacy and romance) change?

- What reasons do people give for saying that premarital sex or living together before marriage is okay?

Has our culture's definition of what love means crept into your thinking or marriage?

The summation of love's attitude has nothing to do with feelings, but everything to do with forgiveness.

Why is forgiveness the epitome of love's attitude?

- Share a time in your marriage when you either offered or received forgiveness and experienced great healing as a result.

Who is the most loving spouse you know? What does that person do that makes him or her such a great example of married love?

- What have you learned from the person that you could incorporate into your own relationship?

Purposeful

Examine yourself. Are you allowing the enemy to have his way in your home? Is unforgiveness in your heart stifling love's attributes, hindering love's allure, and quenching love's attitude?

Take some time and slowly read through 1 Corinthians 13.

- Be honest with yourself as you're reading, and assess how well you are loving your spouse. Journal if it is helpful.

- Spend some time in prayer asking God to help you in areas of need.

Recall things that have hurt you in your marriage. Are you holding on to the pain in unforgiveness? This exercise is not meant to make you angry as you revisit hurts. Instead, its purpose is to reveal to you how much you have even unknowingly gathered hurts one on top of another. Forgiveness is an act of the Holy Spirit in your life. You cannot live under the suffocating burden of unforgiveness. Pretending as if you have forgiven someone will eventually fail; only true Holy Spirit forgiveness pumping through your veins will give you freedom and healing. Denial cannot do that; true liberty in Christ is found only in true forgiveness.

Prayer

Dear heavenly Father, I praise You for the forgiveness You have extended to me. Thank You for loving me personally. I thank You also that You have reminded me of what love truly is. I ask that Your definition of love would reign in my heart, life, and marriage. Help me to continue to be strong and courageous as I press into You for help, healing, and wholeness. I pray You would reveal to me tangible ways that I can be a more loving spouse. Help me to esteem Your Word by honoring it in my life. Repair my heart where it has been broken and my mind where I have misunderstood Your truths. In Jesus' name I pray. Amen.

Chapter 5

THE RULES OF COMBAT

Pride leads to disgrace, but with humility comes wisdom.

— PROVERBS 11:2

It has been said that marriage was made in heaven, but then so are thunder and lightning! For many couples, the clouds of marital discord soon gather on the horizon after they say "I do," and the calm of the honeymoon quickly becomes more like a hurricane. This catches many off guard, and if we don't know what to do about it, we can draw some illogical conclusions, like "I guess I married the wrong person." No, it is not likely you married the wrong person. You just need to learn what to do when your honeymoon cruise goes through a hurricane and the inevitable disputes of life arise in your marriage. It doesn't mean your marriage was a mistake or you made the wrong choice. It simply means you're normal and human, and two becoming one is going to take some getting used to. That's what this chapter is all about.

Many factors contribute to stress in the home. These stresses lead to communication problems that result in the forsaking of good manners. Remember what 1 Corinthians 15:33 says: "Evil communications corrupt good manners" (KJV). Financial stresses, work pressures, family issues, and even health challenges can all precipitate strain in a marriage. If we're not careful, we can begin blaming and turning on each other at the time when we need each other the most. This is one of the enemy's most successful traps that snare many couples: allowing life's pressures to become marital stresses.

I want you to pay close attention to this chapter. If you're one of those fortunate couples who always seem to see eye to eye—and to be honest, I have met only one among the hundreds of couples I have married or counseled—the principles shared in this chapter will equip you to help others who struggle in their marriages. If you're married but struggling to live in peace and harmony, know that you can learn how to resolve your differences in an acceptable manner. If you're single, the information presented will prepare you for healthy interaction with your future spouse as well as provide you with a way to evaluate the ability of someone you're dating to deal with conflict in a satisfactory way. There's truly something for everyone as we take a look at how to handle the disruptions that threaten the harmony in our homes.

Avoiding Conflict in the Home

In an earlier chapter, we took a look at Proverbs 29:11: "A fool vents all his feelings, but a wise man holds them back" (NKJV). If we all lived by that one verse, it would prevent a lot of problems from arising in the first place, wouldn't it? But that is not reality for most of us. When a disagreement arises between a husband and a wife, feelings and emotions often dictate the course of the conversation and the attempts at resolution. Feelings are difficult to hide; even if we don't say a word, our body language and facial expressions often betray our true feelings. If we could look back on our lives and note all the comments we made in response to hurt feelings, we would discover this is the primary reason for discord that turns into combat.

Some of the hurt feelings that emerge from husband-wife interaction can be traced to the basic differences between men and women. However, we seem to forget that fundamental principle and instead expect our mates to behave the way we would behave in a given situation. A humorous story illuminates that thought:

A wife was making breakfast for her husband when he suddenly burst into the kitchen and shouted, "Careful! You need more butter. Oh my gosh, you have too many eggs in the skillet at once! Turn them—turn them now!"

His wife looked at him, puzzled by his outburst. Before she could make any comment, however, he began again: "You need more butter. The eggs are going to stick. Careful . . . careful . . . I said be careful! You never listen to me when you're cooking—never! Hurry up and turn them, and don't forget to salt them. You know you always forget to salt them. Use the salt, use the salt, use the salt!"

The wife was understandably rattled and stared at him with a hard look. "What in the world is wrong with you?"

she demanded. "You think I don't know how to cook a couple of eggs?"

To that the man calmly replied, "I wanted to show you what it feels like when I'm driving."

We've all experienced something like that, I'm sure. We are quick to dispense advice, so sure our way is the right way, the only way, and fail to take into account that our mate's way of doing things may be just as valid. It's only different, that's all. This is true of many aspects of human relationship, but especially in the close environment of the home. It is imperative, therefore, that we learn how to deal with these differences and not permit them to become a matter of contention in our homes.

Disagreements will always be a part of any human interaction, and that is certainly true of the relationship between husband and wife. The goal of never having an argument is certainly admirable, but hardly attainable. To learn how to deal with disagreement constructively and how to express ourselves in an acceptable manner in the heat of the moment is a more profitable and reasonable tactic.

Pride as the Root of Conflict

There are many facets of conflict resolution that we could look at, but I've selected three rules of combat to discuss that I think are particularly applicable to the marriage relationship. Before we look at these, however, we need to stop a moment and examine the true source of all marital discord — pride. It is the root of all ungodly behavior, including those negative actions that sometimes manifest in the conflicts that arise between those who have entered into the most sacred of covenants. That's why it's so important to remember this first major point:

Wounded pride is the root of most marital discord.

I once heard a preacher say, "You can't be humbled if you already are." That's a true statement, to be sure. We all know Proverbs 16:18, "Pride goes before destruction, and a haughty spirit before a fall" (NKJV). Pride is the root cause of most problems and issues, so if we can learn how to crucify it before it rears its ugly head in our marital relationship, we will be well on the way to discovering the secret of marital bliss and harmony.

We have visited the subject of male-female differences throughout our chapters, but we also need to mention differences in personality types as well. Not everyone handles life the same way, and since life includes conflict, not everyone handles conflict the same way. But the goal does not change, even as personality types seek to learn how to communicate more effectively with each other. Be humble, and resolve conflicts quickly and reasonably.

Someone once said that a woman has the last word in any argument. Anything a man says after that is the beginning of a new argument! You may laugh at that, but we all want to get in the last word in an argument. But the problem is, two people both having to have the last word turns a conflict into a never-ending story and inevitably leads to one person saying hurtful things that provoke the other person to counter with even more hurtful things. When emotions take over and dictate the course of the conversation, we are soon locked and loaded in the "ready, fire, aim" mode of communication. We are "ready" with emotional responses because we have to "fire" back with the "aim" of self-defense instead of sound conflict resolution. When feelings are hurt, self-control often flies out the window. If men and women would only learn how to communicate instead of retaliate, much of this could be avoided.

When you're facing a situation where your pride has been hurt, the first thing to remember is that pride is a characteristic of the flesh, never an attribute of the Spirit of God. When your pride is wounded, stop and take note that you are exhibiting the first symptom of getting into the flesh. Then do something spiritual in order to combat the desire of the flesh.

Answer this question honestly: have you ever stopped to pray in the middle of a conflict? I don't know about you, but it's hard to stay "fleshy" when you are conversing with the creator of the universe. We have all heard the adage "fail to plan and you have planned to fail." With that in mind, I have often counseled couples to sit down and formulate a written strategy for conflict resolution, especially when this area has been a struggle for them. I'd like to encourage you to do that too.

Start by setting *alert levels* in your conflict-resolution strategy. These will help you to recognize developing conflict. Then insert *prayer points*, where you stop and pray about the conflict, and *pause points*, where you give each other some space before discussing the problem. Be careful with these pause points. Set a specific time limit to cool off and a definite time when you will come back together to discuss the issue. If it takes days for either one of you to cool down, then you are not managing your frustration well or have deeper pride issues that are causing anger-management malfunctions.

Do not allow your communication to be ruled by emotions and pride, but by the Spirit and truth. Again, if this one issue is recognized and confronted honestly by a good long look in the mirror, you will be able to avoid the vast majority of problems that arise in your home.

It goes without saying that husbands and wives ought to avoid hurting each other's feelings and wounding each other's pride at all costs, but we also recognize that basic male-female and personality differences often cause it to happen anyway. For some couples, there is always something to fight about. Feelings are so raw and pride so wounded that the smallest thing can set one of them off, and they can't seem to agree on anything. What do you do in a case like that? Again, check your pride, recognizing it as a work of the flesh. Like most things that are worthwhile, this is easier said than done, but remember, if you aim at nothing, you are sure to hit it. When a repetitive cycle of feelings-based outbursts is a pattern, there is no question that the proper solution has not been attempted.

My wife and I have long adopted the practice of examining everything that is said to us for any element of truth—even if what was said was intentionally meant to hurt us or was a "chocolate dagger" offered by one who "only wants the best for us." We also employ this same strategy in our relationship with each other. Yes, hurtful things are said to all of us, but learning how to handle them should be birthed out of learning how to do so at home.

I am of German descent, and my wife is of Irish. To say we are both strong willed and stubborn would be something we would argue with you about! The reality is that sometimes hurt feelings mask accepting something that really needs to be addressed. This self-confrontation thing is risky business, to be sure, but the rewards far outweigh the risks. No matter the method or the messenger, the way to lay down our pride and handle our end of conflict resolution is to ask ourselves, "Is there any truth in what was said to me?"

The other side of this is to identify your own motive in what you are saying during an emotional exchange: "Is what I am about to say factual, or is it feelings based? Is there a possible positive result to be gained by saying this, or is winning the only thing I am concerned about?" The acronym THINK would be fitting here. Before you speak, consider whether what you are about to say is True, Helpful, Inspiring, Necessary, and Kind. This is a great filter for every exchange, especially when emotions enter the arena of conversation.

The Rules of Combat

Now let's move on to the three rules of combat. Pay close attention here, and be ready to take these to heart. Here's the first rule:

Rule #1: Past failures are off limits during a current conflict.

In Isaiah 43:18-19, God said to rebellious Israel, "Do not remember the former things, nor consider the things of old. Behold, I will do a new thing, now it shall spring forth; shall you not know it? I will even make a road in the wilderness and rivers in the desert" (NKJV). Although this was spoken to Israel, remember, Israel is referred to as God's wife and the church as the bride of Christ. With that in mind, it is not a stretch at all to apply these words to the marriage relationship.

One of the reasons so many couples seem to engage in a repetitive cycle of combat is found in verse 18: they do not forget the former things but continually dredge up every one of their mate's past failures. That, however, is in direct contradiction of what we seek for ourselves from God. As Psalm 25:6-7 emphatically reminds us, "Remember, O Lord, your compassion and unfailing love, which you have shown from long ages past. Do not remember the rebellious sins of my youth. Remember me in the light of your unfailing love, for you are merciful, O Lord." How can we ask this of the Lord in regards to our personal shortcomings yet refuse to extend the same kind of mercy to others, especially to our mates? Isn't this that pesky Golden Rule found in Matthew 7:12: "Do to others whatever you would like them to do to you"? Far too often the rule is amended to read, "Do unto others before they do unto you."

This is a fatal flaw if it is part of your conflict resolution. You might want your spouse to really try to see your point of view, but are you really trying to see theirs? You might wish they would stop doing that thing they "always do" when a conflict arises, but have you stopped doing what they say you always do? Let your expectations dictate your actions. Do *for* your mate what you want *from* your mate, and watch how quickly you resolve conflict.

When communication breaks down into verbal combat (I am purposely using aggressive language here because for some that's how conflict resolution seems), the very first thing you must remember is to keep past offenses in the past. Resist the temptation to use them as fuel on an already raging fire. When facing a conflict in your marriage, dragging in the past is strictly off limits. In other words, fight about what you are fighting about. The past is not an arsenal of weapons for your current battle.

Singles, beware the man or woman who continually brings up every little wrong thing you do or constantly corrects you. Remember, you're looking for a mate, not a mentor, and this is a sign of things to come for you, should you proceed in the relationship. Let me insert a little balance here for you literal thinkers. It isn't that we can't learn from each other — because we can — but "each other" is the operative here. If you feel like you're dating an instructor instead of an equal, you'd better hit the brakes for a while lest you find yourself playing the part of a lifetime student.

Let Go of the Past

"Do not remember the former things. . . ." There's no room for statements like, "You always say that," or "I knew you would do that because that's what you did last time." Saying things like that reveals much more about you than it does about your mate. It shows you're violating the first rule of combat by keeping a record of past wrongs. If, in fact, repetitive behavior that legitimately needs to change pops up during conflict resolution, bringing it up during the conflict is a bad idea and will bear no fruit. Be wise, and pick a good time to talk about it. Even then, if you come together and find your spouse is not ready to talk, back off and wait for another opportunity.

Please understand, I am not talking about abusive behavior. That needs to stop immediately, and help should be sought right away. I am talking about the general life stuff that all couples deal with, but don't always deal with well. Let the former things die—just let them go. If you find that you and your spouse are constantly fighting about the same thing, first examine yourself for pride. Then check to see if you are fanning the flames of conflict by refusing to let go of the past.

We would all do well to ponder the words of Philippians 3:13-14: "I focus on this one thing: Forgetting the past and looking forward to what lies ahead, I press on to reach the end of the race and receive the heavenly prize for which God, through Christ Jesus, is calling us." This is a toughie to consider here, but it must be done. Forgetting the past includes anything that has been forgiven, repented of, and not repeated—even the big stuff. If there was a breach of trust and God placed it in your heart to forgive, then that too is off limits in resolving a current conflict. Think about this: God doesn't bring up your forgiven past, and you are called to act like Him. So friend, as you heal from any major trauma in your relationship, though you may never forget it, resist the urge to use it as a weapon when discussing something that has nothing to do with that failure from the past. Run the race of marriage by forgetting the past and pressing on to the future. That's the only way to live. When you willingly adopt this practice, your wilderness will be watered by graciousness and mercy, and your times of combat will resolve a lot more quickly.

Now let's move on to the second rule of combat:

Rule #2: Arguing over opinions is a foolish endeavor.

It has been said that any marriage that can withstand the building or remodeling of a house can withstand anything. There is an interesting aspect to that statement that will help us to understand our second rule of conduct. When couples are building a house, their verbal sparring usually follows a predictable pattern. Seldom is the arguing over the type of wood to use for the studs, the thickness of the slab to be poured, the construction of the roof sheathing, or similar considerations. In other words, couples seldom argue about the structural foundation of the house, but they do argue over the cosmetics of the house: the kind of carpet to lay, the color of paint for the walls, the style of cabinet knobs for the kitchen, the best use for a bonus room. But when a storm rages and the wind blows fiercely, none of those things matter. What matters is the structural integrity of the house, the foundation upon which it is built.

Jesus spoke of this in Matthew 7:24–27: "Anyone who listens to my teaching and follows it is wise, like a person who builds a house on solid rock. Though the rain comes in torrents and the floodwaters rise and the winds beat against that house, it won't collapse because it is built on bedrock. But anyone who hears my teaching and doesn't obey it is foolish, like a person who builds a house on sand. When the rains and floods come and the winds beat against that house, it will collapse with a mighty crash." That applies so aptly to marriage. If the foundation is sure, the marriage will weather the storms of life. If the foundation is lacking or weakened by a constant emphasis on trivialities, the stability and long-term sustainability of the marriage are threatened.

Dealing with Differences of Opinion

In my years of doing marital counseling, I have discovered that couples fight over just about anything, but most of it is a difference of opinion. Just as the cosmetics of a house are mostly a matter of taste and preference, many of the issues that arise in marriage have nothing to do with the foundation but deal instead with relatively unimportant externals. Couples fight over TV shows, musical taste, hair color and style, clothing, and a myriad of other things that are a matter of opinion. I find it fascinating that someone can get angry over another person's color preference and think that because their spouse likes a certain color over their own personal favorite, there is something wrong with their mate. Yes, there's something wrong, but not with the mate. How can someone be wrong about an opinion? It doesn't make sense, yet it happens every day. Let me repeat it again: *fighting over opinions is a foolish endeavor.* Instead, let Proverbs 12:15 be your guide: "Fools think their own way is right, but the wise listen to others."

The godly man or woman allows for differences of opinion and respects the right of their spouse to see things differently. My wife, for example, has seen innumerable versions of *Pride and Prejudice*, and I have watched some of them with her. I may have no idea of the movie's allure to her, but I am not going to fight with her for liking it . . . unless she hassles me for liking *The Three Stooges*, that is! Listen, friends, we will come a lot closer to doing marriage right and avoiding marital conflicts if we will simply lay down our pride and allow our mates to be who they are.

Philippians 2:3-4 offers some good advice: "Don't be selfish; don't try to impress others. Be humble, thinking of others as better than yourselves. Don't look out only for your own interests, but take an interest in others, too." If we were to consistently follow those words, we would save ourselves a lot of time and trouble, especially when it comes to matters of personal interest or taste.

A note to the singles here: Finding someone who likes everything you like and thinks exactly like you think is not the answer to avoiding a strife-filled relationship. Differences add flavor to our relationships if we learn how to handle them in the Spirit instead of the flesh. A spouse's differences can become a great blessing if they give us the opportunity to stretch and grow as we learn to accommodate another person. And that's a good thing.

I am a creature of habit. I like to do the same thing over and over and am comfortable with predictable routine. That applies to my eating habits as well. I could eat chicken four or five days a week, throw in a hamburger or steak here and there, enjoy a hot dog or Chinese food on occasion, and be perfectly happy without ever trying anything else. My wife, however, is more adventurous in her culinary pursuits, and because of her, I now enjoy Greek, Persian, Indian, Egyptian, and Thai food—all things I would have never pursued without her gentle prodding. That's what I mean by allowing your spouse's differences to stretch you in your areas of opinion or taste.

My wife also has a great affinity for decorating. Many times I have walked into our home and thought, "Is this our house? Wasn't that over there, and wasn't it a different color yesterday?" I remember sometimes thinking, "Why does she always need to be painting? I was just getting used to the walls this color, and now she tells me she is going to be painting again!" I finally came to the realization that it's just paint. If my wife likes to paint, then I need to let her paint. If she doesn't like the result as much as she thought she would, it's just paint, and she can redo it. Again, to get uptight about the source of another person's pleasure or interest is foolish. We all have our areas of interest, and husbands and wives do not have to both like the same things. (I do have to say I am glad my wife came around on liking football, though!)

So, we have the first two rules of combat: (1) past failures are off limits during current conflict, and (2) arguing over opinions is a foolish endeavor. Let's move on to the third and final rule of combat, and I'll introduce it with a story:

A couple had been arguing all day and finally resorted to the silent treatment. Neither would speak to the other, both hoping the other would break first. As bedtime approached, the man recalled that he had an early flight to catch the next morning. The alarm clock, however, was on his wife's side of the bed, and he wasn't sure if he would hear it. Not willing to be the one to humble himself and break the silence, the man came up with a plan to give himself the upper hand. He smugly wrote a note and left it on his wife's pillow. It read: "I have an early flight in the morning. Please wake me up at 5:30." Quite pleased with his ingenuity, he went to bed.

The next morning the man woke up to the sun glaring through the window. He leaped out of bed and looked at the clock. It was 7:45. Furious, he turned to his wife to break the silence and lay in to her, when he saw the note on his nightstand: "Wake up, honey. It's 5:30 a.m."

Dear friends, there are times when pride creeps into our marriage and communication degrades. But we must never allow ourselves to get caught up in the cat-and-mouse game of the silent treatment. That's rule number three of our rules of combat:

Rule #3: The silent treatment is a tantrum, not a technique.

No Place for the Silent Treatment

When I make reference to the silent treatment, I am not talking about an agreed-upon cooling-off period that may be needed after an emotional exchange. I am talking about giving your spouse the cold shoulder, a prolonged period of ignoring your spouse, giving one-word answers, or speaking short phrases in a disrespectful tone—in a word, pouting. We all recognize it. The silent treatment has no valid place in any marriage, especially a Christian one. Remember what Colossians 3:16–17 says: "Let the message about Christ, in all its richness, fill your lives. Teach and counsel each other with all the wisdom he gives. Sing psalms and hymns and spiritual songs to God with thankful hearts. And whatever you do or say, do it as a representative of the Lord Jesus, giving thanks through him to God the Father."

Speak to your mate in a spiritually uplifting manner, and give no room for the devil to gain a foothold. That means not going to bed without speaking: "Be angry, and yet do not sin; do not let the sun go down on your anger, and do not give the devil an opportunity" (Eph. 4:26–27, NASB). Even if all you say before going to bed is that you will discuss the matter more respectfully in the morning, do it. To simply go to bed without speaking or making any attempt at resolution is to give place to the devil.

Think about this: Have you ever had something go wrong with someone at work on a Friday and had all weekend to think about it? By the time Monday rolled around, you had replayed in your mind a multitude of scenarios as to how this would play out. Maybe you heard something negative or said something negative and wondered how the first face-to-face was going to go, and all weekend long, your mind concocted all types of reasons for you to be angry. Then, when Monday finally came and you returned to work, the whole thing played out in a completely different manner. We have all been there in some form or another, letting our minds run away with us. What allows this to happen? The absence of dialogue.

Friends, going days without speaking to your mate is just flat-out disobedience to godly conflict resolution. Be angry, but do not sin with corrupt words or fighting over matters of opinion. Be angry, but do not sin by giving each other the silent treatment. In any conflict, be the first to offer a soft answer that will turn away wrath (Prov. 15:1). Don't turn a minor altercation into a battle that makes you miss the plane to recovery.

As Romans 12:18 says, "Do all that you can to live in peace with everyone." Remember, though, peace is not the absence of conflict. Peace is what you can have *in the midst* of conflict.

"What percentage of marital conflicts could be avoided?" you may ask. "One hundred percent!" I answer. What percentage will we actually avoid? That depends on you and me. The main problem is pride, the original sin. It was and continues to be Satan's sin, and he easily afflicts us with the same. Pride is literally at the heart of every sin, so if we can eliminate pride, we can eliminate many of our problems. Even when we fail in this endeavor, we can still set the rules of combat into play and shorten the length of the battle.

As we wrap up this section, let me point out how important this chapter is, especially to young married couples today. We live in a world that has been slowly chipping away at distinctions, not just between the sexes, but also in individuality. Two distinct people and personalities enter into a marriage, but contrary to popular opinion, having a happy marriage does not require the death of individuality. It just requires tools to enable us to handle our differences.

Love, in this postmodern age, seems to be the willingness to accept anything and everything that anyone does. The trend seems to be to eliminate conflict by blurring distinctions between the sexes and between individuals. But this is a crime against the beauty of diversity that the infinitely creative God instituted. When differences are recognized and honored, there will be conflicts that must be resolved decently and orderly, but where distinctions are removed, conformity and the death of individuality are all that's left. Remember, young couples, you are fearfully and wonderfully made as individuals; in marriage, God makes the two of you one.

Never forget, humility is the key for godly conflict resolution: "For those who exalt themselves will be humbled, and those who humble themselves will be exalted" (Luke 14:11). Let God be exalted in your home by extending to your mate the same grace that you have received. Even when you don't see eye to eye, give it a shot; you just might learn something and grow as a person as well. I have experienced this in my own marriage, and I know it can happen for you, even after poor conflict resolution in the past.

When you face conflict in your marriage—and you will—remember the rules of combat. First, leave the past out of the present conflict. Deal only with the issue at hand and nothing more. Second, never, under any circumstances, wander into fighting over opinions; that's a foolish endeavor. You do not have to like the same things as your spouse and think the same thoughts in order to get along. Your differences can expand your character and even add spice and interest to your marriage. Third, do not let the sun go down on your anger. The silent treatment never cures a problem; it only creates more. These are the rules of combat. These are the ways to deal with conflict and discord. These are the ways to ensure that you will live happily even after a dispute with the mate of your youth.

Questions for Discussion

Principle

When your honeymoon cruise goes through a hurricane and the inevitable disputes of life arise in your marriage, it doesn't mean your marriage was a mistake or you made the wrong choice. It simply means you're normal and human, and two becoming one is going to take some getting used to.

Personal

Proverbs 16:18 says, "Pride goes before destruction, and a haughty spirit before a fall" (NKJV).

How is pride the root of all marital conflict?

What happens when marriage partners refuse to budge in order to protect their pride?

What is the answer to pride in conflict resolution?

Why is it so hard for many of us to let go of the past when dealing with our spouses?

What are the dangers in constantly bringing up failures from the past?

- How do you feel when someone won't let you forget your past?

- How do you think your spouse feels when you do the same?

Explain the difference between facts and opinions.

- Why do couples get caught up in arguing about opinions?

- How can you allow your spouse to have different opinions from yours without feeling threatened by it?

Why do you think the Bible speaks so clearly about not letting the sun go down on your anger?

- Share a time when you obeyed this scriptural command, and tell what happened.

- Now share a time when you did not obey the command, and tell what happened.

What are some practical ways that gender, personality, and individual differences can make a couple stronger rather than tearing them apart?

Purposeful

Write down the three rules of combat, or rules of fair fighting, and place them where you can easily see them.

1. Leave the past out of the present. Fight about what you're fighting about.

2. Do not fight over opinions.

3. Do not let the sun go down on your anger.

Read them often.

Follow them always.

Prayer

Dear heavenly Father, I want to thank You for my marriage. Thank You that when we do things Your way, it never fails. I ask that You continue to strengthen me as I commit to doing my marriage the right way. I ask You to help me remember the principles of fighting fair and to seek what's best for my marriage by honoring Your Word. I ask that You reveal to me areas that I personally need to grow in. I desire to be pleasing to You. In Jesus' name I pray. Amen.

Chapter 6

IN-LAWS OR OUTLAWS?

This explains why a man leaves his father and mother and is joined to his wife, and the two are united into one.
— GENESIS 2:24

A couple had a fight that led to each of them giving the other the silent treatment. Night passed, and neither spoke a word. On the way to church the next morning, they drove silently down a country road for several miles. As they passed a barnyard with a corral full of mules, the husband decided to break the silence. Turning to his wife, he sarcastically commented, "Relatives of yours?" Without missing a beat, the wife calmly replied, "Yes, my in-laws."

You may laugh at that story, but there's a lot of truth to be gleaned from it. When two people join in marriage, they are joining not only themselves but also their families for life. Different family traditions, practices, and values come into play and must be dealt with. If you add to that the many blended families there are today, the complications can be doubled. For any marriage to be successful, couples must find a way to reconcile the differing outlooks and expectations of their families. As they work out solutions for financial problems, communication weaknesses, and the tendency of pride to appear, they must also confront the battles and struggles that rise from melding two different sets of opinions, tastes, and traditions from their respective families.

As we learned in the previous chapter, arguing over opinions is unwise, yet far too many couples embark on a foolish journey that would be easily curtailed by a more humble approach. Unfortunately, it doesn't always work that way. Take the issue of holiday traditions, for example. Many young couples are surprised when they find themselves locking horns in this arena. Both have brought into the marriage certain family traditions, things that are fond and familiar, that make the holidays feel like the holidays. When their first major holiday season as a unit arrives, each expects to honor their family's long-standing traditions. This assumption is often furthered by the parents who feel the same way, thinking that their traditions will be passed on to this new household. If this doesn't happen, a family rift may develop. The new member of the family is now viewed as an adversary rather than an addition to the family, and in-laws suddenly seem like outlaws.

As fallen human beings, we don't always choose the right path, and sometimes in a marriage, the couple discovers that they do not like each other's family or their traditions and do not wish to be around their in-laws. Instead of the extended family becoming a source of joy, it becomes a wedge in the couple's relationship. Because of the tension and strife in the family, holidays and special occasions are robbed of the blessing they are meant to impart.

My brothers and sisters, this should not be! That's why I've written this chapter. We all need to learn how to live in peace and harmony with our spouse's family of origin. And let me point out that this is a two-sided coin. Both husband and wife have families, so both become in-laws after saying "I do." Both must learn to invest the time and effort it takes to create a genuine bond of love with new family members. Remember, different isn't wrong — it's just different.

Leaving and Cleaving

First Peter 4:9 instructs us, "Be hospitable to one another without grumbling" (NKJV). The word *hospitable* is interesting in that it means "having a love for strangers." This is essential to understanding how the extended-family element of marriage is to be approached. People who were once acquaintances are now members of the family and as family expect to have a say in familial decisions. But again, real-life doesn't always follow the path of what is best, so in this chapter we are going to take a look at four main areas that create grumbling in our families and cause in-laws to sometimes seem like outlaws.

Before we do that, however, let's go back to a familiar verse, Genesis 2:24. Though we have looked at this verse several times already, it is as relevant for this aspect of marriage as it has been for the others. Understanding the divine design is essential to our topic in this chapter, so let's go back to the Garden of Eden and start our discussion there. Genesis 2:24

reads, "This explains why a man leaves his father and mother and is joined to his wife, and the two are united into one." Note that the verse says a *man* will leave his father and mother, much as we saw the scriptural admonition for husbands to love their wives directed to the man and not the woman. The reason, I believe, is much the same. It's not that women aren't called to leave their families, but the point is being made that the husband must cut the childhood ties that bind him to the past so that he can assume his rightful place as head of a new household. As long as he is mentally still a child in his parents' home, he will not be able to do this.

May I also say that the blurring of gender lines in our day has done much to undermine the sanctity of marriage and the home. It has created much confusion for both male and female as they attempt to establish a new home, and the fruit of that is seen in many children today. Let me also point out something I have previously mentioned: marriage and family are divine creations, and what God initiates He also orchestrates. In other words, He has set down principles in His Word to allow for maximum blessing for His people. If your goal is to go with the flow and adopt the world's perspective on marriage, you are free to do so. However, God's blessings are found only within God's boundaries.

One more thing before we press on: Moms do not make good dads, and dads do not make good moms. We are genetically predetermined to excel at certain tasks, and while there is some degree of latitude, the rules as a whole are true. I am not saying that all women must stay home. The Proverbs 31 woman was creative and industrious and obviously possessed a keen head for business, as she oversaw manufacturing and real estate transactions. (By the way, did you know that Proverbs 31 was written by a woman to her son?) God's plan is best, friends, and if you want your marriage to be all it can be, don't accept society's lie that traditional marriage is antiquated and out of touch. Back to our topic . . .

The Hebrew word for "leave" in Genesis 2:24 is *azab*, which means "to loosen" or "to relinquish." The Hebrew word for "joined" (or "cleave" in the King James Version) is *dabaq*, which means "to cling or adhere to." The meaning of Genesis 2:24 is simply that a man will leave his parents and take his place as head of a new home. He will cling to his wife and provide the covering for a new creation, a new family that he and his wife will bring into existence. Nowhere in Scripture do we see the wife given this same natural capacity, but she is exhorted in Colossians 3:18 to submit to her husband. Both have God-given instructions to follow and roles to fulfill if they are to successfully master the art of "leaving" and "cleaving."

That brings us to the first major point of this chapter:

The marriage covenant creates new descendants,
not new dependents.

This does not mean that the new family created by marriage is on its own or disconnected from the extended family. It does not mean that the parents have no influence or input with the new couple. Certainly, there is a time when it is appropriate for parents to help struggling young couples, either financially or personally, though always bearing in mind that the new husband is now the head of a new home and is responsible for being its covering before God. Not father-in-law, not mother-in-law, not dad, and not mom—the husband alone bears this responsibility.

Establishing a New Home

A man who has relinquished his former covering and become one with his bride has stepped into his God-ordained role. The woman who submits to her husband as the head of their home sets the stage for marital harmony in accordance with God's plan. Together husband and wife create new descendants as they waive their dependence on their families of origin. They give birth to a new home that will establish its own customs and traditions and possess its own likes and dislikes.

The actual transition to this God-given design is not always easy. Some tension and misunderstanding are to be expected as all involved become accustomed to their new roles. Parents need to remember that their child's home won't be perfect when it becomes just like theirs. No, the young couple needs to be free to like and dislike in matters of taste without a critical spirit from either side of the family. Parents must learn how to let go of their married children, and the children must learn how to separate from their parents while still showing honor to them. When push comes to shove, however, the young couple's commitment must be to each other above all else. That means, men, when your mother and wife clash, your loyalty lies with your wife. And ladies, when your husband and a family member are at odds, your first responsibility is to your husband. Remember, he left his family to cling to you, so you must do the same for him.

That is not always easy to do, especially for women. The separation from parents and the creation of a new home generally come more naturally to men because God has given them a natural capacity to relinquish and adhere. Women, however, do not inherently possess this quality, so it is natural for them to hold more tightly to their original families and to struggle to separate. Ladies, because of your nature, you may not find it easy to surrender the ties to your family, but Scripture calls you to submit to this. As Proverbs 14:1 points out, "A wise woman builds her home, but a foolish woman tears it down with her own hands." You are going to have to exercise discipline in honoring the new home God called into existence when you said "I do."

Once a new home has been established by marriage, the parents are not to be the sounding board for marital struggles. Young couples need a mature Christian friend or counselor to help them in those areas. Far too many disputes with in-laws are self-inflicted by a husband or wife who tells their family of their mate's failures. The parents are naturally inclined to take their child's side—sometimes even over truth—and their child's spouse is faced with a situation that is difficult to overcome. That is not to say that a young couple must suffer silently or that parents are completely off limits for seeking wisdom and counsel, but only that the young couple must above all else honor their new home created by covenant.

Do you remember what we talked about in our chapter on communication, that the things you say about your spouse to your coworkers ought to plant in their minds that it would be a privilege to meet and get to know them? Apply this now to your family. If you, young ladies, are always telling your dad what a slob your husband is, what do you think he is going to think of him? Young men, if all your mother hears from you is how your bride doesn't do anything right, then what is Mom going to think of her? This underscores the importance of having a good church family and unbiased third parties to discuss things with who will not be tainted by blood ties and natural favoritism.

Young couples, you must find balance in this, of course. Keep in mind that the way your family looks at things or handles certain situations is not necessarily the right way. Be open to learn from your spouse's family. Parents-in-law, if you want to avoid the in-law–outlaw syndrome, let your kids create a family of descendants dependent on God, not on you. They are going to make mistakes, but God has not appointed to in-laws the role of spotlighting them, but of picking their children up and helping them "fail forward," always showing love and respect for the new household and those trying to figure out how to do marriage right.

Romans 12:18 contains some excellent advice for all of us: "If it is possible, as much as depends on you, live peaceably with all men" (NKJV). Notice the first four words: "if it is possible." Sometimes you can do only so much, as evidenced in the following account:

A young man came home and excitedly informed his mother that he had fallen in love and was going to be married. He said, "Just for fun, Ma, I'm going to bring over three women, and you just try to guess which one I'm going to marry."

The mother agreed to the test, so the next day he brought home three beautiful young women and sat them down on the couch. After they all had chatted for a while, the young man turned to his mother and said, "Okay, Ma, guess which one I'm going to marry."

The mother immediately replied, "The one in the middle."

The man responded, "That's amazing, Ma. You're right. It's the one in the middle, but how did you know?"

"I don't like her," came the mother's cryptic reply.

Sad, but true, this too often seems to be the case in many family relationships. My wife Teri and I have had some laughs watching the movie *Monster-in-Law*. It's the story of an overbearing mother who thinks no one is good enough for her son and does everything she can to make him break up with the woman he thinks is the perfect mate. I am sure many would find the movie too much like real life to see any humor in it, but the story does have a happy ending. I also believe that by following God's plan, a happy beginning is possible as well.

Living in Family Peace and Unity

One of the things I love about Scripture is its relevance to real life. The Old Testament has a story that fits perfectly at this juncture. Read it with me:

> While they were at Hazeroth, Miriam and Aaron criticized Moses because he had married a Cushite woman. They said, "Has the LORD spoken only through Moses? Hasn't he spoken through us, too?" But the LORD heard them. (Now Moses was very humble—more humble than any other person on earth.)
> So immediately the LORD called to Moses, Aaron, and Miriam and said, "Go out to the Tabernacle, all three of you!" So the three of them went to the Tabernacle....
> The LORD was very angry with them, and he departed. As the cloud moved from above the Tabernacle, there stood Miriam, her skin as white as snow from leprosy.
> —NUMBERS 12:1–4, 9–10

How many times have families divided over a man's or a woman's choice of a mate? Too many times to count, for sure. But remember, love is indeed blind (and sometimes I have wondered if it is deaf and dumb as well), but barring the choice of a nonbeliever for a spouse, love and beauty are in the eye of the beholder. Far too many times future in-laws become outlaws from the get-go because of their ill-advised criticism of their child's choice of a mate. When faced with this scenario, we need to remember the next truth:

> *Demanding a choice between spouse and family is always the wrong thing to do.*

This is a twofold truth, applying equally to parents and their adult children. Parents who demand children to choose them over their spouses are asking them to sin. Married people who ask their mates to forsake their families of origin rather than do all they can to live in peace with the extended family are wrong too. Whether by implication or insinuation, by direct proclamation or indirect communication, it is always wrong to set up a showdown between spouse and family. It is the wrong way to act and the wrong thing to ask, without exception. Of course, sometimes there are instances when the strife in a family becomes so great that the only wise thing to do is to create some distance, but that is generally the result of wrong already done.

James 3:13-18 provides some sage advice:

> If you are wise and understand God's ways, prove it by living an honorable life, doing good works with the humility that comes from wisdom. But if you are bitterly jealous and there is selfish ambition in your heart, don't cover up the truth with boasting and lying. For jealousy and selfishness are not God's kind of wisdom. Such things are earthly, unspiritual, and demonic. For wherever there is jealousy and selfish ambition, there you will find disorder and evil of every kind.
> But the wisdom from above is first of all pure. It is also peace loving, gentle at all times, and willing to yield to others. It is full of mercy and good deeds. It shows no favoritism and is always sincere. And those who are peacemakers will plant seeds of peace and reap a harvest of righteousness.

This is never more true than in the family and perhaps again best illustrated in the struggle so many young couples face of trying to keep family members happy during the holidays. In this age of blended families, it is not unusual for a young couple to have four or five stops they are expected to make on any given holiday. Carefully they must balance whose house they go to first, how long they stay, and how to schedule the other required stops. Many blessed events have been turned into family feuds because of the pressure of trying to please everyone.

Being the father-in-law of a most wonderful daughter-in-law, I can attest to you that this is not always easy. Like most people, I want my family together on holidays, honoring our traditions as much as possible. But part of the reason I have such a wonderful daughter-in-law is that she came from a wonderful family who loves their traditions too. Both families have had to make adjustments to accommodate this new family. It hasn't always been easy to coordinate our activities, but it has always been worth it.

Of course, not everyone has the good fortune of having Christians or loving and peaceable members on both sides of the family. Some do have that blessing, but the parents are still having a hard time letting go. Still others feel like their mate's family is a bunch of outlaws who are out to rob them of peace and happiness. Regardless of the scenario, if all parties involved would take to heart the scriptural admonition to live at peace as much as it depends on them, personal opinions and demands would take a backseat to preserving family harmony. When the command from Scripture is ignored, self-seeking demands lead only to confusion and every evil thing. May we soberly remind ourselves from the lesson of Miriam and Aaron how the Lord regards such behavior.

Developing Healthy Family Relationships

Let's move on to the next truth in in-law relationships:

All the patience and privileges shown to family belong to those who marry in to it.

Countless jokes have been made and TV shows created that zero in on the dynamic at play when a new member comes into the family. We all laugh at the competition between Debra and Marie in *Everybody Loves Raymond* and, for some of you more mature readers (that's a PC phrase for "older"), Meathead's inability to do anything right in the eyes of his father-in-law, Archie Bunker, in *All in the Family*. Though the scenarios are exaggerated, something in them resonates with us as true. Far too often in life, the introduction of a new person into the family is met with friction instead of joy, and sometimes it starts even before the wedding....

Three days before the wedding ceremony, a bride called her mother. In a panic, she lamented, "Mom, I just found out my fiancé's mom bought the exact same dress as you did for the wedding."

The bride's mother was silent for a moment and then answered, "Don't worry, dear. I'll just buy another dress to wear to the wedding."

"But Mom," her daughter protested, "that dress was so expensive. What will you do with it? It's such a waste not to use it."

"Who said I won't use it?" the mother retorted. "I'll just wear it to the rehearsal dinner." (Some of you men may need to ask your wives to explain!)

Already this mother was striving to be a step ahead of her son-in-law's family, and already she was setting the stage for trouble.

Mothers-in-law and daughters-in-law in particular seem to struggle in adjusting to their new roles after marriage. Mom is afraid of losing her place in her "little boy's" life, and the new wife is sometimes threatened by the long-standing bond of affection her husband has with his mother. This does not have to be. Scripture provides us with a poignant picture of a loving mother-in-law–daughter-in-law relationship in the story of Naomi and Ruth.

> One day Naomi said to Ruth, "My daughter, it's time that I found a permanent home for you, so that you will be provided for. . . .
> "I will do everything you say," Ruth replied. So she went down to the threshing floor that night and followed the instructions of her mother-in-law.
> —Ruth 3:1, 5-6

I won't take the time to repeat the entire story here, but I do think it's important to note a couple of things. First, Naomi referred to Ruth as "daughter," and as her "mother," she took it upon herself to do for Ruth all that she would have done for her own biological daughter. Good mothers-in-law do that. They accept the new member of the family as their own and do not set a higher expectation for them than they do for their biological children. The same mercy and grace they show to their children encompass the new member of the family as well.

Maybe some of you mothers recognize yourself as lacking in this area. Maybe you realize that you have been placing heavy expectations on your daughter-in-law or son-in-law that you don't even expect your own children to fulfill. If you have treated the new addition to your family, the spouse of your child, with less patience and privilege than you show your children, how will that young man or woman ever be able to honor you and value your input and instruction in his or her life? Remember the scriptural admonition: you reap what you sow.

Let me address the daughters-in-law for a moment. Young ladies, your husband chose you before God and witnesses and declared that he would cling to you as the only woman in his life. Your mother-in-law is not your enemy. She is not to be treated as the "other woman" competing for your husband's love and affection.

So what is the right way for any in-law to act, whether a parent or a child? The same way a healthy family related by blood acts. There must be no secondary treatment for anyone who becomes a part of the family through marriage. All the patience, privilege, and kindness afforded to blood relatives must be freely showered upon those who join the family through marriage. That means, older women, sow into your daughter-in-law the same love you have sown into your children. And young women, when your mother-in-law does this, learn from her how to walk as a strong woman of God. Then will the truth of Titus 2:3-5 come into effect and positively affect both you and her: "Similarly, teach the older women to live in a way that honors God. They must not slander others or be heavy drinkers. Instead, they should teach others what is good. These older women must train the younger women to love their husbands and their children, to live wisely and be pure, to work in their homes, to do good, and to be submissive to their husbands. Then they will not bring shame on the word of God."

Fathers, too, must learn how to embrace new additions to the family, and this may be particularly hard for them when it comes to their sons-in-law. A father is naturally protective of his daughter and may find it difficult to accept that another man will take his place as his daughter's protector and provider. He is always looking out for his "little girl" and casts a wary eye on any young man vying for her hand. The following story may seem familiar to you:

A nice Christian girl brought home her fiancé to meet her parents. After dinner, the father invited the young man to join him on the front porch for iced tea. "So what are your plans for my daughter?" he asked the young man.

"I am a Bible scholar," he replied.

"Admirable, but how will you provide a nice home for my daughter?" the father queried.

"I will study," the young man responded, "and God will provide."

"How will you buy my daughter a beautiful engagement ring, one that she deserves?" the father persisted.

"I will concentrate on my studies, and God will provide for us," the young man answered again.

Still not satisfied, the father asked, "What about children? How will you support children?"

"Don't worry, sir. God will provide," the young man insisted once more.

The father asked several more questions, and each time the young man answered the same: "God will provide."

Going back into the house, the man was met by his wife, who asked, "How did it go?" to which the man answered, "The boy has no job and no plans, but the weird thing is, he thinks I'm God."

Yes, fathers will do what they must to protect their daughters and help their sons, but Scripture lends better insight into the parent-child relationship and its relevance to our topic. Ephesians 6:1–4 says:

> Children, obey your parents because you belong to the Lord, for this is the right thing to do. "Honor your father and mother." This is the first commandment with a promise: If you honor your father and mother, "things will go well for you, and you will have a long life on the earth." Fathers, do not provoke your children to anger by the way you treat them. Rather, bring them up with the discipline and instruction that comes from the Lord.

Verse 1 is obviously a reference to children in the home. The covenant of marriage creates a new home with a new head, so the married couple is not expected to obey their parents as when they were children living at home. However, they are to honor them, and this command spans the realm of childhood and beyond. Interestingly, the word *honor* in verse 2, which is a quotation of the fifth commandment, literally means "to promote richness." So, adult children, promote richness with your parents and in-laws, for this is right before God.

Verse 4 addresses the responsibility of the father in his relationship with his children, both those at home and those who have married and left home. Fathers are clearly instructed not to provoke their children to anger. In the Greek, the word translated "provoke" is *parogizo,* which means "to anger alongside"; the root word implies "by your proximity." In other words, men, your presence is not meant to create strife and anger in the home of the new family. Your son-in-law is not a "meathead," and your daughter-in-law is no "bimbo." As this text reveals, fathers share the same responsibility as do mothers in accepting their children's spouses and treating them the same as their children by birth.

Fathers, model for your children and their spouses what is right in the Lord. Your example is key to pulling out the best that may lie dormant in that new member of your family. Pay special attention to this final important truth:

No one ever becomes all they can be by only hearing all they are not.

Whether you are dealing with a son or son-in-law, daughter or daughter-in-law, or any other member of your family, never demean. Your responsibility is to honor and love. "But you don't know my son-in-law," you might protest. "He's got so many things he needs to change, and I can help him see that." Well, maybe he does need to change, but your role is not to point that out. Rather, take Romans 2:4 to heart and do what it says: "Don't you see how wonderfully kind, tolerant, and patient God is with you? Does this mean nothing to you? Can't you see that his kindness is intended to turn you from your sin?" Just as God shows kindness that leads you to repentance and transformation, so must you show kindness, tolerance, and patience to your in-laws. That is your primary role.

Does this mean family members can never confront one another about behavior they find unacceptable? No, not necessarily, but caution must be exercised. After all, the Father does correct His children: "For the LORD corrects those he loves, just as a father corrects a child in whom he delights" (Prov. 3:12). The key is whether you are correcting from love or from spite. Correction done for spite is no one's delight, nor is it right before God.

I want to add a word of encouragement to those who said "I do" and with those words created a blended family or, maybe for some, an instant family. Just as favoritism falls naturally along bloodlines when the subject is in-laws, so too does it in the matter of children. Since the family unit of today often includes stepchildren, let me admonish those who have married into this scenario that there is no second set of standards for raising the biological children of someone else. If they are your spouse's children, you said "I do" to treating them as your own—even when they say, "You're not my dad," or "Don't tell me what to do; you're not my mom." Your proximity to them should not stir up anger. In addition, you will need to fight favoritism when or if you have kids of your own.

I recognize that the pain of divorce and the sight of Mom or Dad with someone else are deep wounds to a child's soul, but this gives you all the more reason to be loving and tenderhearted towards a stepchild even though the kindness may not be returned. Remember, this is a child who needs nurturing and love, and you have, though maybe not legally, adopted him or her into your family. *Adopted* is an important word, because we all understand that someone who adopts a child that they have no biological connection to does not do so with the expectation of loving them less or treating them differently from the way they treat one of their own. The blended family is to live under the same loving standards as any other; there is no second set of rules.

Let me close this chapter with a few questions:

Fathers-in-law, are you patient with the young man who has entered your daughter's life as her covering and protection?

Sons-in-law, do you promote richness in your relationship with your father-in-law, or is he the "old windbag" your wife calls Dad?

Daughters-in-law, do you reject the insight and wisdom of your mother-in-law because you view her as overbearing? If so, you are depriving yourself of a rich source of knowledge.

Mothers-in-law, do you accept your daughter-in-law as one of your own, loving her unconditionally while acknowledging that she must be first in your son's life?

To all, are you as patient and long-suffering with your in-laws as you are with your own family? Look deep inside and answer truthfully.

When a new home is established, the man leaves his mother and father and cleaves to his wife. Their loyalty to each other surpasses any sense of loyalty to the families they came from. If this basic principle is understood by both the newly married couple and their families, many of the common problems that pop up with in-laws can be avoided from the start. Never should a man or woman feel as though they come second to their spouse's family, and the one who creates that feeling is out of bounds and their actions bordering on betrayal.

Matthew 5:9 tells us, "Blessed are the peacemakers, for they shall be called sons of God" (NKJV). Division and discord within a family are always from the devil. If they have found their way into your home, examine yourself and see if you were the one who let them in. Dear friends, when in-laws seem like outlaws—or even act like them—someone has not followed God's plan of living in peace. If that is you, purpose today to make peace a priority. Your in-laws can become just as dear to you as your natural family, and you can live happily even after combining two very different families into one. The choice is yours—in-laws or outlaws? Which will it be?

Questions for Discussion

Principle

Together husband and wife create new descendants as they waive their dependence on their families of origin. They give birth to a new home that will establish its own customs and traditions and possess its own likes and dislikes.

Personal

Explain the necessity for "leaving" and "cleaving" when a couple marries.

- What are some of the hindrances to this taking place?
- What role do parents play in helping their newly married children make this transition?

What was your greatest challenge in establishing a new home upon marriage?

- How did you and your spouse resolve it?

How can a couple successfully honor their parents while retaining primary loyalty to each other?

- What do adult children owe their parents, and what do parents owe their adult children, if anything?

For in-laws, why is it so important to treat your children's spouses the same way that you treat your own children?

- What does this look like, practically speaking?

When a new home is established, the man leaves his mother and father and cleaves to his wife. Their loyalty to each other surpasses any sense of loyalty to the families they came from. If this basic principle is understood by both the newly married couple and their families, many of the common problems that pop up with in-laws can be avoided from the start. Never should a man or woman feel as though they come second to their spouse's family, and the one who creates that feeling is out of bounds and their actions bordering on betrayal.

Purposeful

Think about your own individual situation at home:

For parents of children still at home, what could you do to help prepare your children for the day when they will leave to establish homes of their own?

Write down what you could do for your daughter-in-law or son-in-law to enhance their personal growth and help them feel more a part of your family.

Think about and write down what kind of words you speak in all your family relationships.

- Are they uplifting and encouraging, or critical and discouraging?

- If they are critical and discouraging, write next to them what words should be used instead.

Examine your heart. If helpful, journal your thoughts, listing the areas that need to improve.

- After reading this chapter, are there areas you feel really good about? What are they?

- Are there things that you feel could improve? If so, make a list of how to go about making things better from your end.

- Are you committed to having a loving extended family, or are you content to let in-laws seem like outlaws?

Prayer

Dear heavenly Father, I bless You for creating families. Most of all, I thank You that You have placed me into Your family. My heart's desire is to please You, and I ask You to keep me close to Your heart on matters of my extended family. Holy Spirit, continue to guide and strengthen me to be of strong moral character and to be loving toward others. I ask that You bless me with revelation knowledge and the wisdom of Jesus Christ and that in all the issues of life, marriage, and love, I would excel. In Jesus' name I pray. Amen.

Chapter 7

WHEN EVERYTHING GOES WRONG

God blesses those who work for peace, for they will be called the children of God.

— MATTHEW 5:9

We've covered so many aspects of doing marriage right. First, we laid the foundation by explaining that marriage is a covenant relationship between one man and one woman. From that, we moved forward and learned that marriage can be a perpetual honeymoon, that we can live happily even after with our God-given mate. Next, we examined the importance of developing effective communication skills that take into account the inborn differences between men and women. That led us into our study of love as the overriding key to a healthy, joyous marriage, which hopefully will guide us when we face the unavoidable conflicts that come in life. Finally, we took a close look at the rules of combat we need to follow when dealing with confrontation and the importance of a couple establishing a new home of their own while maintaining ties to their families of origin. When those six principles are established in the heart and demonstrated in appropriate action, any marriage is well on the way to being all that it can be as a reflection of Christ's undying love for His church.

But when the potential of marriage is never fulfilled, what do we do? Where does it leave us when we have sought to be the peacemaker in our home, but our every effort has been rebuffed by an unbelieving spouse? Which way do we turn when we have been abused, betrayed, or rejected by the one who was supposed to complete us? I know some of you have found yourselves in a situation like that and are thinking, "Things can never change in my marriage. I'm stuck in this dead relationship." Others of you may be thinking, "The damage is too great to overcome"; or "I made the wrong choice in the first place." In other words, there is a very real question that must be answered:

What do we do when everything goes wrong?

Remember, friends, God is perfect, and so are all His plans, including His plan for marriage. If you will give honest effort to the things you've learned from His Word thus far, you will see change for the better — even if the only change you see is in you. In God's economy, marriage is a holy institution, loved and created by Him. It is not a feelings-based set of contractual obligations that can be freely broken whenever emotions change. It requires hard work, compromise, communication, and a commitment to permanence. Here's a gentleman who understood that clearly:

Satan burst into a church one Sunday, frightening everyone so badly that all but one old man fled from the building in terror. This older gentleman remained calmly seated in the front row.

Puffing himself up to his full stature, Satan got right in the old man's face and bellowed, "Do you know who I am?"

"Yup," was the old man's one-word answer.

"Aren't you afraid of me?" Satan hissed.

"Nope," came the calm reply.

Perplexed by the exchange, Satan demanded, "Why not, old man? Why aren't you afraid of me?"

"I ain't afraid of nothin'," the man responded. "I've been married to your sister for almost fifty years."

That story may make you chuckle, but the sad truth is, some people are married to very difficult people. Not everyone lives in a fairy-tale marriage. Problems are real and sometimes even devastating. So what do you do when everything goes wrong in *your* marriage?

Let me start by saying something that seems so obvious yet needs stating: God is with you in the midst of any problem! Whatever it is, no matter how terrible, God sees and God cares. We have the sure promise of Psalm 147:3-5 to hold on to: "He heals the brokenhearted and bandages their wounds. He counts the stars and calls them all by name. How great is our Lord! His power is absolute! His understanding is beyond comprehension!"

Do not miss the majesty of what you just read. The God who names and numbers the stars, the God of infinite power and understanding, cares about your wounds and even bandages them for you! This is the heart of the Lord for those of you who have seen everything go wrong in your marriage. Don't ever forget it: God cares and desires to be actively involved in healing your pain.

I will remind you once again that I am not writing to you of things I think or things I feel are true. I am writing to you from the position of personal experience. I have seen God take a marriage that could not have been any more dead and breathe life into it and make it into something it never was. He took what I made my marriage into and transformed it into what He intended all along. When two people are willing to cooperate with Him and submit to His plan, there is always hope for beauty from ashes, joy from mourning. These words are not pontification from me—they are my testimony!

Repentance and Forgiveness

Turn with me now to another psalm, Psalm 32. Written by David, this psalm is one of thirteen psalms that bear in their titles the Hebrew word *maschi*. This word means "to give instruction." After David's sin with Bathsheba, a year of silence went by regarding his behavior until he was confronted by Nathan the prophet (see 2 Samuel 12). Following that confrontation, a brokenhearted and repentant David wrote this psalm, a psalm of forgiveness and healing when everything goes wrong. Inspired by the Holy Spirit and penned by the hands of experience, it can be a tool in the hands of the Lord to mend your own broken heart.

In the first five verses of Psalm 32, David gives great insight into what to do when everything goes wrong. Look at the New King James Version with me:

> Blessed is he whose transgression is forgiven,
> Whose sin is covered.
> Blessed is the man to whom the LORD does not impute iniquity,
> And in whose spirit there is no deceit.
> When I kept silent, my bones grew old
> Through my groaning all the day long.
> For day and night Your hand was heavy upon me;
> My vitality was turned into the drought of summer. Selah.
> I acknowledged my sin to You,
> And my iniquity I have not hidden.
> I said, "I will confess my transgressions to the LORD,"
> And You forgave the iniquity of my sin.

David reminds us of where to begin when the failure has been our own. He extols the beatitude of "blessed is he whose transgression is forgiven, whose sin is covered." There is but one way for sin to be forgiven, and that is by covering it. But first we must acknowledge it and repent of it; then we have the assurance of 1 John 1:9: "But if we confess our sins to him, he is faithful and just to forgive us our sins and to cleanse us from all wickedness." Praise God, the blood of Jesus covers our sins! But just as David had to agree with what God said about His sin, so too must we acknowledge our guilt and ask for forgiveness.

Dear friend, you might look back on your life and see times when you have erred. You may have failed miserably and hurt many people by your actions. I know from firsthand experience what that feels like. Sometimes the hardest person to forgive is yourself, especially if everything went wrong during a time when you had strayed from God. Sometimes you think you don't deserve forgiveness, so you never contemplate confessing your sin and starting over.

I have overcome some major battles in my life, and one thing I have learned from doing so is something I often share with others trying to break free from destructive habits or the struggles of the past. Whatever you are facing, overcoming it is not as hard as your mind is telling you it is. When I was struggling with drinking, I remember thinking, "I want to stop drinking, but I know I can't. Lifelong sobriety is just too much to expect. I've gone too far, and I'm in too deep." That is a lie from the devil, friends, and denies the Word of God that I can do all things through Christ who provides strength. This illustration may be specific to an area that I battled, but the application is universal. Nothing is as hard as you think it will be, since Christ is your strength. Now please understand, I am not saying that changing is easy, but I am saying that our minds and flesh try to convince us it cannot happen, which is not true.

I urge you today to fall into the hands of a merciful God and cast all your cares upon Him. He cares for you and longs to bind up your wounds — even if self-inflicted. Take to heart David's words in Psalm 32, and admit your wrong. From those timeless words, the first major point of this chapter is made:

Freedom and healing come through ownership of sin, not blame.

Even if everything going wrong in your marriage was primarily the fault of your spouse, there is still something for you to learn in the difficulty, a way for you to grow. Healing will never come if you wait for your spouse to take the blame, because you cannot control another person's actions. You can control only your own actions, and healing will come only when you take ownership before God of your behavior.

Own Your Failures

I have had many a person in my office over the years whose area of expertise seems to be everything their mate does wrong. My counsel to them is always the same: as soon as you are perfect, you can start working on your mate! Now obviously, this is meant to grab their attention and realign their focus. Couples can and should be agents of change for each other. However, we must understand that none of us have the ministry of running other people down, but we all have the ministry of lifting others up, beginning with our mates. Remember our comment that the words you speak about your mate to your coworkers should create in them an expectation of meeting someone special? That same principle needs to be applied when talking *to* your mate, not just *about* them.

Daniel, one of the elite few in Scripture who is described as without fault (Dan. 6:4), gives us a great perspective on not blaming others for the way our life has played out. As righteous as he was, he refused to waste time blaming others for his life. In Daniel 9:4–5, he prayed: "O Lord, you are a great and awesome God! You always fulfill your covenant and keep your promises of unfailing love to those who love you and obey your commands. But *we* have sinned and done wrong. *We* have rebelled against you and scorned your commands and regulations" (emphasis added). Although he had been only a boy when carried captive to Babylon and had not contributed to the demise of his people, the righteous Daniel identified himself with sinful Israel. He looked deep within and confessed his shortcomings. If you are one those people for whom everything has gone wrong at the hands of another, learn from Daniel.

Maybe what you're facing is your fault, and maybe it isn't. Regardless, the fact remains that owning your failures is the key to freedom and healing—yours, that is. Proclaim with the psalmist, "Have mercy on me, O Lord, for I am weak; O Lord, heal me for my bones are troubled" (Ps. 6:2, NKJV). When everything in your marriage has gone wrong, refuse to take up the yoke of bitterness for things outside your control. Call out to God for His mercy. Refuse to keep silent about your own sin and shortcomings. Silence about your sin is what creates weary bones. Nursing the wound of a failed marriage or constantly contemplating the pain caused by an unbelieving mate will never free you and bring healing to your life. This is a universal truth that must be grasped.

Allowing the deeds of another to dictate the path and attitude of your life is not the way to handle things when all goes wrong. Does that mean you're not supposed to hurt, that you're supposed to move on as though the struggle is nothing more than a bump in the road that will soon be crossed? No, of course not. It does mean, however, that in any given circumstance, even when you have been truly wronged, you take ownership before God of your faults, not waste valuable time playing a blame game in which nobody wins.

Remember, the power to be healed and free lies in ownership, not blame.

Praise God in the Circumstance

Let's go back to Psalm 32 and take a look at verses 6-9, again in the New King James Version:

> For this cause everyone who is godly shall pray to You
> In a time when You may be found;
> Surely in a flood of great waters
> They shall not come near him.
> You are my hiding place;
> You shall preserve me from trouble;
> You shall surround me with songs of deliverance. Selah.
>
> I will instruct you and teach you in the way you should go;
> I will guide you with My eye.
> Do not be like the horse or like the mule,
> Which have no understanding,
> Which must be harnessed with bit and bridle,
> Else they will not come near you.

Here we see the praise of David in verses 6–7, a heavenly promise of guidance in verse 8, followed by a warning from David's experience in verse 9. When everything goes wrong in your life, praise God *in* it—not *for* it. His worthiness of praise has absolutely no attachment to your feelings or personal circumstances. In the flood, in the fire, in the darkest night, God is worthy of praise. When everything goes wrong in your life, join your voice with the psalmist's and say, "Why are you in despair, O my soul? And why have you become disturbed within me? Hope in God, for I shall again praise Him for the help of His presence" (Ps. 42:5, NASB).

The Lord responded to David's praise with a promise of guidance, "I will instruct and teach you in the way you should go; I will guide you with My eye"; and David then warned the reader not to be like a horse or a mule. A mule, as you know, is generally regarded as one of the most stubborn of all animals. So, in this Scripture passage, David is saying to praise God in your circumstance, look for His guidance, and be teachable to receive it. That's a much better strategy than allowing Satan to exploit your pain and keep the wound fresh through blaming and bitterness.

Stay in Fellowship

I have seen many people fall prey to the temptation of isolation when everything goes wrong. They withdraw into a place deep within themselves that affords access to none. This leads me to my second major point:

Loneliness is never conquered by isolation.

I have been a police chaplain for many years and have received some very helpful training in critical-incident and mass-casualty stress management. One of the most effective tools I have learned is to get the victim of a trauma to start talking about the event as soon as possible, even at the scene. The mind has some wonderful built-in defense mechanisms (including shock) that allow us to endure the unthinkable. But the sooner a traumatized person begins to talk about what has happened, the sooner normal cognitive processes are restored. This does not lessen the pain by any stretch, but it does keep the mind working and allows the person to begin the process of moving forward in life with this unwanted and unexpected scar.

If the enemy can isolate you in your pain, he will. The loneliness that follows devastating pain and betrayal sometimes seems unbearable. When everything goes wrong in your marriage, your first inclination may be to draw back, to shut down, or even hide your struggles, not wanting anyone else to know. That, however, is a self-protective mode that will hurt you in the long run because it will keep you from your brothers and sisters in Christ who are singing the very songs of deliverance that you need to hear. In isolation, you are more likely to fall deeper into the blame game, accusing even God Himself for everything that went wrong.

Dear friend, in the day of trouble, do not withdraw and spend your time demanding an explanation from God for what went wrong or why He did not intervene. God has never been the cause or the blame for any marital woe—sin and pride have caused them all. He does not want you to suffer alone. In fact,

Psalm 68:6 says, "God places the lonely in families; he sets the prisoners free and gives them joy." That's what He wants to do for you. Don't let the fact that everything that could go wrong did go wrong define your life. Surround yourself with the body of Christ, and join them in singing songs of deliverance.

I know this is a tall order. There are times when a marriage is brutalized by adultery, and the enemy comes in like a flood upon the unsuspecting spouse. There are times when sin is repented of and forgiven, but the consequences damage the marriage relationship seemingly beyond repair. At those times, it's easy to lock ourselves away and listen to the lies of the enemy. But that is the opposite of what Scripture tells us to do.

Hebrews 10:23–25 says, "Let us hold tightly without wavering to the hope we affirm, for God can be trusted to keep his promise. Let us think of ways to motivate one another to acts of love and good works. And let us not neglect our meeting together, as some people do, but encourage one another, especially now that the day of his return is drawing near." Wow, what powerful words! Did God give this command just to make sure that the church is full? Is this scripture given to the preacher so he can hold it over the heads of the congregation and guilt them into coming into church? A thousand times no! This scripture from the Word of God was given because loneliness is never conquered by isolation. God's people, when going through difficulty, need to be surrounded by songs of deliverance and strengthened through Christian fellowship.

If everything has gone wrong in your marriage, you may have a voice in your head that constantly whispers, "No one cares. You're all alone. You really don't matter. God did nothing on your behalf to prevent this. Stay home. Be alone. It doesn't make any difference. . ." That, dear friend, is the voice of the devil—not God.

There is another great tool we can find in the last two verses of Psalm 32:

> Many sorrows shall be to the wicked;
> But he who trusts in the LORD, mercy shall surround him.
> Be glad in the LORD and rejoice, you righteous;
> And shout for joy, all you upright in heart! (vv. 10-11, NKJV)

Sometimes in life it seems as though the wicked go unpunished. Sometimes it seems as though the wrong, injustice, and violence inflicted on a marriage by one of the spouses creates a life for the other that will never be the same. But as Charles Spurgeon said, "Faith in God is the great charmer of life's care, and he who possesses it dwells in the atmosphere of grace surrounded with a bodyguard of mercies." That's just what David is saying too. When you have been wronged by someone you love, trust in the Lord, and look for His mercy. Be glad, rejoice, and shout for joy, for your God will never leave you alone. Your spouse may fail you, but God never will.

Let me address for a moment the unrepentant wrongdoer. There is a sober warning for the one who is complacent in sin, comfortable with breaking God's covenant. Proverbs 28:13 admonishes, "People who conceal their sins will not prosper, but if they confess and turn from them, they will receive mercy." There is a mentality today that says, "I can do whatever I want in my marriage, and God will just forgive me." That is a dangerous outlook, my friend. Yes, God forgives sin, but only when we confess and turn from it. Confess and turn—two aspects to the forgiveness process.

Matthew 5:29-30 sheds some more light on what we are required to do in this process of confessing and turning: "So if your eye—even your good eye—causes you to lust, gouge it out and throw it away. It is better for you to lose one part of your body than for your whole body to be thrown into hell. And if your hand—even your stronger hand—causes you to sin, cut it off and throw it away. It is better for you to lose one part of your body than for your whole body to be thrown into hell." In other words, if your TV is causing you to sin by neglecting your spouse, get rid of it. If the Internet is causing you to sin by pulling you down the path of pornography, get rid of it. It is better to do without than to exist in a living hell because of it. If you are flirting with someone at work, stay away from them—leave your job if necessary. It's better to be looking for a new job than to be looking for a new spouse because you gave in to sexual temptation.

Thankfully, God does not easily give up on His children. Like any loving parent, He disciplines those who are His: "But consider the joy of those corrected by God! Do not despise the discipline of the Almighty when you sin. For though he wounds, he also bandages. He strikes, but his hands also heal" (Job 5:17-18). If you have been dabbling in sin and wondering why trouble has come into your life, I say to you, "Do not despise the discipline of the Almighty." Yes, He chastens and corrects, but your healing and wholeness are found in your response to Him. If you are the perpetrator in marital discord, confess it to God and turn from it. Quit living on the edge of sin and destruction, and come fully into God's camp. Don't wait until God has to take measures — sometimes extreme ones — to correct you. This, too, is the voice of experience speaking.

Joy Comes in the Morning

I love how the Word of God is applicable to every life situation. It is true for all of us in any situation we face. It is true for the ones who have been offended at the hands of their mates, whose spouses have been unfaithful or abandoned them. It is true for those in whose marriages everything has gone wrong, and though they have prayed and sought God, no relief is in sight. It also holds true for people like me who are haunted by poor decisions and actions taken before we knew Christ or while we were prodigals, the consequences of which we live with daily. Wherever you find yourself as you read this chapter, know this:

A joy that transcends every sorrow is waiting for all who believe.

When we have been wronged, we may be tempted to take pleasure in the punishment of the wicked, but that is not of the Lord: "I take no pleasure in the death of wicked people. I only want them to turn from their wicked ways so they can live. Turn! Turn from your wickedness. . . . Why should you die?" (Ezek. 33:11). Do you hear the heart cry of God? Does it match your own, or have you been allowing bitterness to replace compassion and mercy in your heart? Knowing the sorrow that awaits the wicked is no source of comfort for the truly converted.

Let me close this chapter with a word picture: Imagine for a moment that you receive a certified letter stating you are the only heir of a distant relative who has left you an inheritance of several million dollars. The next day you receive in the mail late notices for numerous bills and turnoff dates for your utilities; because of circumstances beyond your control, you fell behind on all your financial obligations. What significance will the certified letter play in the way you handle the situation? Well, you are fully aware of the problems you face, but you know without a doubt that help is on the way.

The same holds true for those of you today who say that everything has gone wrong in your life. Romans 5:6-9 is the "certified letter" you've been waiting for: "When we were utterly helpless, Christ came at just the right time and died for us sinners. Now, most people would not be willing to die for an upright person, though someone might perhaps be willing to die for a person who is especially good. But God showed his great love for us by sending Christ to die for us while we were still sinners. And since we have been made right in God's sight by the blood of Christ, he will certainly save us from God's condemnation." Before everything went wrong in your life, Jesus Christ made everything right! Mercy will surround you, and shouts of joy will fill your mouth again.

Remember where we started at the beginning of this chapter, Psalm 147:3-5: "He heals the brokenhearted and bandages their wounds. He counts the stars and calls them all by name. How great is our Lord! His power is absolute! His understanding is beyond comprehension!" If everything has gone wrong in your life—whether by your doing or someone else's—the Lord God of heaven who numbered and named the stars wants to bandage your wounds. The question is, will you let Him?

Deep wounds always leave a scar. The imprint and impact of everything gone wrong can stay with us a long time—even lifelong sometimes. But friend, because of what Jesus has already done, one day you will have a new body with no scars. You will live with your Savior forever, and everything that was wrong will be made right. Hold tight to that and never forget it.

In the meantime, in this earthly life you live, how do you face today when everything in your marriage has gone wrong? First, take ownership for your part in the problem. Freedom and healing will never be found if you refuse to look at yourself and only blame your spouse for the breakdown of your marriage. Second, by no means can you allow the enemy to draw you into isolation, away from the fellowship of other believers. Remember, isolation is never the cure for loneliness. And finally, set firmly in your mind that there is a joy that transcends every sorrow you will face in your marriage. If the answer does not come in this lifetime, it will in the next.

Marriage is one of life's greatest joys and, for some, one of life's greatest sorrows. It is a covenant ordained by God Himself, eternally sanctioned in the heavens. It is a God idea, not a man-made one. It really is possible to live like a honeymooner with the mate of your youth. Years pass and circumstances change, but a couple committed to living their marriage God's way retains the flame of youthful love. They have honed their communications skills and used them to make their bond stronger. Above all, they have clothed themselves with love and learned the secret of melding two families into one. And when the storms of life come—and they surely will—they have learned the secret of turning to God when everything around them seems to be going wrong. This is the couple who has discovered how to do marriage right. This is the couple who has mastered the art of living happily even after. This may not describe you right now, but do marriage right and it can be. Only believe!

One closing thought before continuing or restarting your romantic God ordained adventure through life as a married couple. I know that not everyone reads the introduction portion of books they read and if you did not please take time to do so for it is there I want to take you back to. As King David penned the words of the Holy Spirit we were reminded of what is true concerning all of God's plans; they are perfect! If you are one of those that think that things can never change let me encourage you and remind you that it is not possible for your marriage to be excluded from the benefits and blessings of God's plan if you and your spouse, or perspective mate, are willing to follow it. That thing about Gods word not returning void in Isaiah 55:11, is still true, even for you!

It is possible to live happily ever after "even after" things have all gone wrong, I know its true because it is our testimony and can be yours too! May the Lord bless you and your marriage as you seek to do marriage the way God has intended.

May you, as two imperfect people, enjoy the richness, romance and beauty of the perfect plan of an all knowing God who gave to humankind, the "fix" for the one thing in all of creation that was not good, marriage.

Blessings to you as you "do marriage right" and may you live Happily... even after!

Questions for Discussion

Principle

God is with you in the midst of any problem. Whatever it is, no matter how terrible, God sees and God cares. We have the sure promise of Psalm 147:3-5 to hold on to: "He heals the brokenhearted and bandages their wounds. He counts the stars and calls them all by name. How great is our Lord! His power is absolute! His understanding is beyond comprehension!"

Personal

Have you ever played the blame game in your marriage when facing a problem?

- Did it solve anything?
- What is the better, more scriptural way of dealing with marital issues?

What is the key in dealing with your mate when you really and truly are the one who has been wronged?

What is the difference between praising God *for* a circumstance versus praising Him *in* a circumstance?

- Which are we called to do, and how does it release God's power to work on our behalf?

Have you ever isolated yourself from others when facing a big problem? How did it affect you and others?

- Why is Christian fellowship so necessary when you are having problems in your marriage?

- Share a time when you opened yourself to others and they were able to help you with a problem in your marriage.

When you are going through a difficult time in your marriage, it often feels as though relief will never come. But sooner or later, the trial will pass and joy will be restored.

- Describe a time when this happened in your marriage, and share how your marriage was stronger for having gone through the trial.

Purposeful

If you have ever experienced or are currently experiencing a difficult time in your marriage, take some time to think about a few things. Journal, if helpful.

Have you taken ownership for your part in the problem? Freedom and healing will be difficult to experience if you refuse to look at yourself, even though your spouse may bear most of the responsibility for the breakdown or problems in your marriage.

Taking an honest look at your situation is not intended to be a condemning exercise, but rather one that helps you see actions or decisions that contributed to the situation. Once those things are identified and you see them and own them, you can move towards changing, with the desired end of not repeating the negative behavior.

Have you allowed the enemy to draw you into isolation, away from the fellowship of other believers? Remember, isolation is never the cure for loneliness. If your answer is yes, mark on your calendar the next Sunday, midweek, or Bible-study service, and make plans to go. Make it your goal to be with other believers who can surround you with love and fellowship.

Set firmly in your mind that there is a joy that transcends every sorrow you will face in your marriage. Be mindful of your self-talk. If it's wrong, change it. Speak life, scriptures, promises, and truth over your own life and into your heart.

Prayer

Dear heavenly Father, thank You for Your love for my marriage. Thank You for reminding me there is hope even when all has gone wrong. I ask for Your pure wisdom as I move forward in life and in my marriage. I ask for strength and power to do Your will and a willing heart to obey Your Word as my heart and marriage heal. Thank You for Your plan and purpose for my life, and may my life and marriage be a testimony of Your love and healing power. In Jesus' name I pray. Amen.

CPSIA information can be obtained at www.ICGtesting.com
Printed in the USA
LVOW05s1003290713

345114LV00002BA/2/P